RAISING FUNDS WITH FRIENDS GROUPS

A How-To-Do-It Manual for Librarians

Mark Y. Herring

HOW-TO-DO-IT MANUALS FOR LIBRARIANS

NUMBER 128

NEAL–SCHUMAN PUBLISHERS, INC.
New York, London

Published by Neal-Schuman Publishers, Inc.
100 William Street, Suite 2004
New York, NY 10038

Copyright © 2004 by Mark Y. Herring

All rights reserved. Reproduction of this book, in whole or part, without written permission of the publisher, is prohibited.

Printed and bound in the United States of America.

The paper used in this publication meets the minimum requirements of American National Standard for Informational Sciences—Permanence of Paper for Printed Library Materials, ANSI Z39.48—1992

Library of Congress Cataloging-in-Publication Data

Herring, Mark Youngblood, 1952–
    Raising funds with friends groups / Mark Herring
        p. cm.—(A how-to-do-it manuals for librarians; no. 128)
    Includes bibliographical references and index.
    ISBN 1-55570-484-0
    1. Library fund raising—United States. 2. Friends of the library—United States. 3. Public libraries—United States—Finance. 4. Academic libraries—United States—Finance. I. Title. II. How-to-do-it manuals for libraries; no. 128.

Z683.2 .U6H47 2004
025.1'1'0973—dc22

2003044266

DEDICATION

For Allene,
Ingenio maximus

CONTENTS

Preface vii
Acknowledgments xi
Chapter 1   Understanding the Value of Friends Groups 1
Chapter 2   Getting a Friends Group Started 17
Chapter 3   Establishing the Friends Executive Board 29
Chapter 4   Catching the Web 41
Chapter 5   Marketing Your Library 57
Chapter 6   Communicating With Your Membership 75
Chapter 7   Maximizing Advocacy and Support 91
Chapter 8   Programming a Friends Event 105
Chapter 9   Scrutinizing Your Market 119
Chapter 10   Perpetuating Friends 131
A Friends Group Starter Kit
     A. Creating Effective Bylaws and a Constitution ..145
     B. Spelling Out What the Friends Group Will (and Will Not) Do 159
Index 165
About the Author 167

UMass Dartmouth

PREFACE

Ten years ago, I wrote *Organizing Friends Groups* for Neal-Schuman's How-to-Do-It Series. When it came time to update that book, I first imagined that it wouldn't be more than a matter of a chapter or two of new writing with a few additional features. I should have realized that the enormous changes in the topography of other areas of the library landscape over the last decade would also apply to the important subject of friends groups. I came to realize that today, a truly useful book on friends groups should include all the fundamentals about forming and maintaining a group, but it must focus on the increasingly essential area of fund-raising. The result is *Raising Funds with Friends Groups: A How-To-Do-It Manual*.

In the past, most groups thought that raising a few hundred, or even a few thousand, dollars would be more than enough to ensure the financial future of the library. So why has fund-raising now become so increasingly the crucial *raison d'être* of friends groups? While it is true that libraries have always faced some financial difficulties, none were as dramatic or as widespread as those we see today. Libraries face serious financial challenges, including: sky-rocketing inflation, the wholesale cancellation of serial titles, and the ability to collect in both print and Web-based materials. If friends groups were once underutilized as a key fund-raising tool, many administrations, reacting to the real world, financial bottom-line of their organization, now encourage any group associated with the library to generate the much-needed funds that enable their institutions to thrive.

Raising Funds with Friends Groups: A How-To-Do-It Manual focuses on all libraries but it issues a special call to academic libraries to seek out friends groups with greater vigor and zest. Public libraries do this well and those of us in academic library settings would do well to learn from them. After all, in this country, there are tens of thousands of all types of libraries; however, there are not tens of thousands of friends groups.

One goal of this book is to move those predisposed to forming groups to initiate them at long last. I have covered the indispensable information about successful ways to start and maintain a group where none exist. Throughout, I attempt to address these challenging questions:

- After you organize a friends group, how can this group actually raise funds?

- If you wanted to raise significant resources, what must you do?
- How must you configure your friends group to meet these resource challenges in the most effective manner?
- If a group already exists, how might you retool it for increased fund-raising purposes?

CHAPTER HIGHLIGHTS

- Chapter 1, "Understanding the Value of Friends Groups," offers the sound essentials of why you should bother to build the group in the first place. It identifies the variety of groups, explains how they solve problems, and describes the role of FOLUSA—Friends of Libraries U.S.A.

- Chapter 2, " Getting a Friends Group Started" examines the basics of organizing a new friends group and suggestions for initial success. It includes ways to "think big," the role deans or directors might play in the process, and the seven important rules not to violate.

- Chapter 3, "Establishing the Friends Executive Board," shows you how and why a successful group starts from the top down. It describes the four strengths board members should bring to the group, the qualities of an ideal member, and places to find him or her. This chapter looks at the role of "glad-handing," the best ways to conduct an executive board meeting, and finally cultivating the "three c's" of an executive board: clout, conviction, and closure.

- Chapter 4, "Catching the Web," shows how using the Web enhances the fund-raising capabilities of friends groups. It examines good communication concepts by looking at the best of more than a dozen outstanding sites. It also explores concrete ways that a Web site can help a friends group raise money, including thinking of the site as an ever-present member available to "talk" to anyone, as a place to accept contributions—even run a store!

- Chapter 5, "Marketing Your Library," advocates making the library it represents the centerpiece of any friends group. It stresses the value of friends knowing as much about the library as possible, to become their best ambassadors. It also sounds a clarion call for marketing libraries in general—something we can all learn to do more. It explores the why and how of "selling" services, resources, and successes as winning fund-raising tools.

- Chapter 6, "Communicating with Your Membership," may be the one key to creating flourishing friends groups. It spells out the purpose of soliciting funds and seeking new members. It looks at communication: the differences between formal and informal communication; and the need for keeping them frequent, well done, persuasive, and varied. This chapter takes into consideration both conventional means, such as newsletters, and some not-so-conventional means, such as e-zines, Web sites, and even blogs.

- Chapter 7, "Maximizing Advocacy and Support," emphasizes the critical role advocacy groups play in the well-being of libraries. It explores the different kinds of advocacy, how to select members, levels of advocacy, and becoming media savvy.

- Chapter 8, "Programming a Friends Event," explores the best ways to present the annual (or biannual, or monthly) event that will bring in additional funds, as well as new members. How do you match the events to the mission of the group? How do you decide on the event—its timing, locale, theme, publicity, research, and budgeting?

- Chapter 9, "Scrutinizing Your Market," examines how to conduct reliable, approachable feasibility studies. Learn about the market, its extent, what it will bear, and the potential for various types of projects. Learn about the warnings, as well as, the benefits of these studies.

- Chapter 10, " Perpetuating Friends," shows how to keep your group going. If starting a friends group is hard, keeping one going may be harder still. Chapter 10 draws on research and then compares those findings to three groups that have been around fifteen or more years.

"A Friends Group Starter Kit" includes two key documents. The first outlines the contents of what a bylaws statement should have and reprints bylaws from several groups to aid the Friends Coordinator in creating bylaws if none are at hand. The second summarizes what the Friends Coordinator needs to be aware of when starting a group. Think of these as the dos and the don'ts of friends groups formation.

Each chapter closes with a box called "At a Glance" reinforcing the main ideas of each chapter. These act as a checklist and can even be used as a *Raising Funds with Friends* blueprint to follow step-by-step.

FOLUSA, the Friends of the Library U.S.A., is also showcased here. While it is not in every chapter, its presence is a given throughout. It is rare when starting such an endeavor to have such great resources at hand. Those friends groups that begin and end with FOLUSA will never be disappointed. Those that do not may not be around long enough to realize why they didn't succeed.

Establishing or reinventing your friends group is a worthwhile venture. Focusing on raising the funds that will help your library reach its greatest goals is an exciting and vital enterprise. It can also be a great pleasure.

ACKNOWLEDGMENTS

No book ever gets written by one person. The great bard, Samuel Johnson, is said to have quipped that a man will turn over half a library writing a book. I would add that he will also go through a whole community of friends, well-wishers and acquaintances. I am not at all sure that it takes a village to raise a child; but I know for a fact that it takes a town of friends to write a book. I am indebted to many, so permit me to thank them now.

I begin at the beginning and that is with my bosses, my immediate supervisor, Tom Moore, our Vice President of Academic Affairs (and his predecessor Melford Wilson), and the president of Winthrop University, Tony DiGiorgio. Tom took over as vice president as this book drew to a close and I thank him for his support. He is already a faculty member's best friend and advocate. Winthrop University is fortunate to have him in that post, coaxing and cajoling all of us along. His predecessor, Melford Wilson, held that position for most of the writing of this book. Melford is a raconteur par excellence. My work with him for the last three and one-half years was both instructive and delightful. Melford encouraged me throughout and to him I owe a heart-felt thanks.

I credit Winthrop's stature as one of the state's premier teaching institutions to our president, Tony DiGiorgio. He put Winthrop on the map and established it as one of the state's highest achieving institutions, not because we all think so, but because so many third party assessments have confirmed its status, as such—Winthrop is the *only* institution in South Carolina that can boast 100% accreditation for all programs that have nationally accrediting boards. As a teaching institution, at Winthrop research is important and respected, but it is not primary. Nevertheless, not only has Tony supported it, but has tripled the research funds available to faculty to pursue their research interests. It is one thing to say you support something, quite another to fund it. Tony has done both for Winthrop, in addition to making it a stellar place to work.

I could not have done this work were it not for the able help I have on hand at Dacus Library. I like to think Dacus is one of the state's best because of the excellent library faculty and staff we have on hand. Camille Livingston in Access Services, what we once called interlibrary loan, came on board as I began writing, and I want to single her out for the able assistance she provided in finding literally scores of articles and citations. Amid the other 3,000 or so requests she fills each year, she also filled mine, on time and right on the mark. Many thanks, Camille, for a job very well done.

I work with two of the best executive specialists at Winthrop, Bessie Meeks and Dot Barber. Dot handles all of our accounting business in Dacus, but fortunately for me she also gets called upon to do extra duty. Not once during this process did she complain (she never does about anything!) when called upon to track down something for me and this book, though it is really beyond the scope of her duties. It also helps that Dot has worked here at Dacus more than thirty years, and so had much to teach me when I came here four years ago. Thanks a million, Dot.

Bessie Meeks left her teaching duties at a local high school to join us two years ago. It just so happened that she had used her talents to train the minds of literally hundreds of Rock Hillians in how to write. The felicities of phrasing here the reader may see are hers. I take sole responsibility for those words and phrases that may grate on the reader, for they are doubtless where I failed to follow her excellent advice. Bessie read through the manuscript at least twice, and some chapters three and four times. She often did this at nights and on weekends, all for no extra pay. I highly value her skill and proficiency.

Of course all the library faculty and staff contributed something to this book, if nothing more than putting up with my moods when things were not going as well as I hoped. I must, however, single out one person in particular—my associate dean, Larry Mitlin. Larry has been a mainstay at Winthrop for more than thirty years. He did much to relieve the burden of duties on more than one occasion when I needed to meet deadlines. Not many deans in this country have the luxury I have of being able to meet those deadlines and not once be bothered, because the "shop" is in such capable hands. Moreover, as our technology guru, Larry gave his excellent advice for several chapters in this book.

I would be greatly remiss if I did not thank my editor, Michael Kelley at Neal-Schuman. Michael is that rare editor who has nothing but a writer's best interests at heart. Everything he said or did was done to make this a better book. Of course, any faults are my own. But the advantages you see in this book are owing to Michael's gentle insistence. While writing books over my career, I have had numerous editors and I have been, for the most part, very fortunate. But none have been so beneficial to me as Michael. Not only were his suggestions, recommendations, and changes always on the mark, but I know for a fact that they were done for one reason: to make this a more readable, better book. Moreover, Michael also knew just when to praise and when to cajole. I'm sure this is something for which he is known to all those who are fortunate enough to have him as editor. But it means so very much when your editor takes the time out to call you and tell you just how right something is, or how well this or that turned out. He kept touch with this process throughout and I can only express my heartfelt thanks to him now.

My wife of three decades, Brenda Carol Lane, makes writing books (this is now my sixth) such an easy task, it seems at times a crime to keep imposing them on her. I don't know how others are able to do it without such an excellent helpmeet. She, too, has taught English in the public and private schools where my career has taken us. She has read portions of this manuscript and it is so much the better for it. Moreover, she has been the mother of our two daughters, now grown, and for that my lifetime is too short to praise and thank her enough.

Finally, there is Allene Stuart Phy-Olsen, to whom this book is affectionately dedicated. Allene is scholar of merit, from whom I had the pleasure to learn as an undergraduate. Allene is one of those rare professors whose breadth and depth of knowledge has no equal. I owe my education to Allene, to her insistence to make my meanings clear, to her infectious love of knowledge, to her encouragement and faith in me, and, most of all, to her friendship for the last quarter century. I don't know if she remembers this, but I also owe to her my very presence in this profession.

While working on an NEH grant twenty-plus years ago, I feared for my future. The grant would end and then what would I do? My dream of becoming a medievalist was not to be. With a wife, a young daughter and another on the way, there simply was no way I could drop out of the job market for six or seven years and acquire the necessary training. While working on the grant with me, Allene suggested I look into library science. As she so astutely pointed out, I could remain in academe where I seemed destined to land, continue to research and even write, while also fulfilling an important role as librarian. It is so typically prescient of her that it worked out just as she said. I can think of no one more deserving of my gratitude. Were it not for her, it is unlikely I would have ever written this book, or the other five, or any of the scores of articles and reviews I have authored over the years. Austin-Peay State University is most fortunate to have her, sharing her prodigious knowledge of literature and scholarship. I am most fortunate to have known her, both as a scholar, and as a friend.

1 UNDERSTANDING THE VALUE OF FRIENDS GROUPS

FRIENDS GROUP—WHY BUILD? WHY BOTHER?

Pick up any newspaper and read for yourself the troubling economic times we now face. Enron went belly-up; ditto that for WorldCom. Dozens of other dot-coms that made their employees millionaires one year, made them paupers the next. Meanwhile corporate executives are accused of insider trading, Martha Stewart has allegedly done a not so good thing after all, and the Dow loses about fifteen percent of its value in *one* business week. Public and civic organizations curtail, cut, rescind, scale back, furlough, and regroup.

Double the Prozac, because that's just the beginning. Pick up any issue of the *Chronicle of Higher Education* and you will read a second verse, echoing the first. In Tennessee, state government (including all its university libraries) shut down briefly in the summer of 2002. Alabama, its neighbor, makes draconian cuts in the state budget. Georgia wonders if the funding of its scholarship program is in jeopardy (it is), while Virginia cuts all state programs across the board. Iowa, normally a bellwether state free from budget vacillations, is cutting is educational programs right and left. Meanwhile, South Carolina required its colleges and universities to return nearly ten percent in 2001, took back eight percent in 2002, and has now ordered all agencies to reduce overall funding by yet another ten percent in fall 2003. Almost no state is safe; nearly all are in some form of state budget free-fall.[1]

The question you are probably asking at this point is, "What has this got to do with libraries in general and what, especially, does this have to do with friend groups in particular?" The answer is a simple one: only everything.

BROTHER, CAN YOU SPARE A DIME?

The obvious point is that by now many librarians at every kind of library—public, private, special, academic, or school—have experienced severe budget cuts first hand. Some have cut or furloughed personnel, while others have cancelled periodical subscriptions, or reduced book budgets. Of course none of this is new. Libraries have fallen on tough financial times since, well, since forever. In the history of library funding, there has never been an Age of Pericles, a Golden (Midas) Age, unless we point to that one brief shining moment in the middle fifties and early sixties. Since then, it has been an uphill battle. Moreover, this is *not* an overnight development; it has been going on for *decades*. Prices for materials in public libraries have not decreased, though relatively speaking the serials crisis left some untouched. Nevertheless, all costs for public libraries moved dramatically upward, while budgets shrank nationwide. Since 1992, *academic* library materials have gone up more than one hundred forty-five percent.[2]

Stop and think about that number for a moment. When health-care costs went up sixty-five percent, we had a national hand-wringing over it. Health care rushed to critical mass so quickly that some even tried to bring a failed political idea to this country: socialized medicine.[3] Has there been any hand-wringing over libraries? Does anyone know about the crisis, other than librarians?

THE FAULT, DEAR BRUTUS, LIES IN US

The answer of course is no. Part of that is our own fault. Librarians are good at recognizing the problem, but not so good at trumpeting its solution other than the bromide: give us more money. Paraphrasing Mark Twain, library budgets are like the weather: everyone talks about them, but nobody ever does anything about them. What *really* amazes us is that the economic fiasco in libraries has persisted for at least two decades, and not only have librarians done little about it, but also many librarians, especially at institutions of higher learning (where I work), still do not "get it." Public library friends groups are flourishing. Special libraries friends groups have almost always been a feature of the organizations to which they are attached. But *academic library* friends groups? They still number in the few hundreds though the institutions themselves number in the thousands.

Given these dreadful economic times, one might be led to ape a popular commercial as an interrogative to all librarians: "Can you hear me *now*?" With looming financial crises and cuts coming from every quarter, hitting the heart of libraries, this ad slogan has special meaning to libraries today.[4]

If all of this were not enough, consider: the variety of friends groups is endless. There are small groups, large groups, groups that meet once a year, and groups that meet once a month. Friends groups supply funds for books, capital improvements, periodicals, rare books,

> Paraphrasing Mark Twain, library budgets are like the weather: everyone talks about them, but nobody ever does anything about them.

> "Can you hear me *now*?" With looming financial crises and cuts coming from every quarter, hitting the heart of libraries, this ad slogan has special meaning to libraries today.

manuscripts, equipment, advocacy *and all of the above*. Sure it is hard work, but not nearly as hard as figuring out which magazines to cut, which programs to axe, or which people to "downsize." With every reason to have a friends group, with financial revenue streams drying up at the state, local, and federal levels, and with every possibility for any type of group limited only by the imagination, why haven't more librarians, especially academic ones, availed themselves of them? Several answers to this question come to mind, many of which will be answered throughout this book. One answer can be given straightaway: it is definitely *not* because there are no paradigms. While the examples of academic friends groups may be limited, there are enough examples out there in all types of libraries to render this excuse simply a poor, ill-informed one.

HOLY FRIENDS GROUPS, BATMAN

Take, for example, the Emmanuel School of Religion (ESR), located in Johnson City Tennessee. With a faculty and staff of less than 150, the friends groups there, made up largely but not exclusively of faculty and staff, have managed to build one of the more impressive religion collections of its kind. Students who attend there are definitely *not* hampered because the library is very small. Judging by the volume numbers alone, the library would have to be classified as tiny. Yet, judging its contents, students of the ESR library have the opportunity to sample *primary* works of religious scholarly materials that are probably not available at schools twice its size. All of this is courtesy of a kind of ad hoc friends group that pours money into the library coffers annually. And this occurs only because some enterprising librarian made it his business to make sure the problem was known to his small constituency and the remedy carefully and fully explained.[5]

The Friends of the Simsbury Public Library in Connecticut supply volunteers and offer special programs in addition to financial assistance. The Friends of the Santa Cruz Public Library support the library through advocacy, volunteers and fund-raising.[6] The Friends of the Library at North Carolina State University have a magnificent program that involves buying Rare Books, holding program events and hosting an annual book sale. It has been in operation since 1947 and "fosters understanding and appreciation of the Libraries' role in promoting the academic excellence of the University."[7]

Some librarians may feel that they have to compose some grand and dramatic verbiage that will electrify patrons. If you read between the lines you come away with the incontrovertible idea that lies at the heart of all friends groups: *When you help the library, you're not helping one student or one discipline or one person; you're helping every student, all disciplines, every patron.* It's hard to come up with anything better. Just think about it. Hardly any other financial opportunity allows so much for so little. Help the library and you help every student who comes through the institution, every citizen in that community, *and beyond*. What could possibly be more electrifying to a would-be donor than this? *It's a win-win proposition.*

> When you help the library, you're not helping one student or one discipline or one person; you're helping every student, all disciplines, every patron.

COMPOUND INTEREST

Davidson College, located just north of where I live, is an elite private school where parents know well-ahead of time that they will be paying considerably more than any state institution's tuition. Yet even there, money is still an issue. Leland Parks, the director of the library for nearly three decades, began a program more than two and half decades ago that allowed anyone to donate five hundred dollars and books would be purchased for the library every year, in perpetuity. The program still pays dividends today. In fact, the largess is mind-boggling: today the fund stands at six million dollars.[8] When created, books cost about five dollars each and so the program built a huge principal early on. Today, a similar fund might require two thousand dollars or more to achieve the same advantages. Even so, the "program" requires some staff time, and reports of the donations are made just as much an essential part of giving as endowed chairs.

What makes it work is the genius behind compound interest. There are no programs, no events. No "big galas." Instead, with some effort on the part of staff, the book and periodical funds of Davidson are guaranteed success every year, even in very tight financial times such as these. What makes the Davidson program even more remarkable is that the funds are *budget enhancing* not budget relieving. This is a point worth noting now: set up your program from its inception to be budget enhancing, excluded from your annual operating budget, and get it in writing. Too often such programs become a sincere temptation for others to "raid" when times are tough, or worse, to remove library funds for other programs. That the Davidson program has remained faithful to its constituents is not only a testament to a well-orchestrated program, but also to all the people at Davidson College who honor its perpetual existence.

FRIENDS OF THE TOMPKINS COUNTY PUBLIC LIBRARY

The friends group of this public library, located in Ithaca, New York, have a dramatic story to tell. In the fall of 1991 the library purchased an eleven thousand square-foot warehouse. In May of 2002, several volunteers came together for the "Burning of the Mortgage" party that the *friends group paid off*! Through book sales and other events this small but extremely active group provides positive proof that a friends groups can do anything. They have nearly two hundred fifty volunteers, who work more than fourteen thousand hours annually to pull off incredible feats.

TEXAS-SIZED

At the Friends of the Sterling C. Evans Library at Texas A & M University, the group "provid[es] the extra margin to help the library meet the growing needs of students and faculty."[9] In 1970, Mr. Evans began the friends program and since that time it has aided the library chief mission. The program also boasts that it "combines 'friendraising with fundraising'."[10] Students there can join for ten dollars annually, "Associates" at fifty dollars, while "Sustaining Friends" join at the one hundred dollar level. "Fellows" join at the two hundred fifty dollar level. "Patrons" and corporations may enlist at up to nine hundred ninety-nine dollars each. "Benefactors" are recruited at one thousand dollars and up. Note the various categories. Only two are really small. The rest of the categories place "serious" contributors in logical giving arenas. Many programs nickle and dime the library to death. Oftentimes, enterprising libraries, eager to "get something underway" offer just about anything. Only later do they learn that when the time element is factored in, the dollars earned are quite small in comparison to the hours required to make the program work. In the end they find they have worked too hard for too few dollars and the library is not only financially no better off, but volunteers (and library staff) are exhausted with keeping the program running.

Texas A & M Friends have a number of activities, including an annual "Fun Run." The 2001 event occurred in February (obviously only a town located in the extreme South could offer this in the dead of winter) and prizes (medals) were awarded to the top three finishers in each age category. Some librarians believe that every program must be a cerebral exercise but Texas A & M proves this isn't necessary. Judging from the photographs posted on the Web page, more than one hundred participants enrolled in the race. The event is fun, festive and showcases the library at every turn. Is the friends group successful? You be the judge: it garnered nearly nine thousand dollars in additional funds.

MISHAWAKA

The Friends of the Mishawaka-Penn-Harris Public Library began in 1980.[11] The group offers programs, its own "Bittersweet Book Sale" and its "Hi-Lites" newsletter. The group also offers a "writers' support group" that encourages local writers as they hone their craft. Not only are there the usual categories of gift support, but they also offer family memberships, "Junior" levels for K-12 grades (for only one dollar). What an excellent idea to get children to understand the importance of libraries, not only as a resource, but also as something *they* can support. Various volunteers provide programming for children and others.

MORE READ IN O-HI-O

The friends group at Ohio Wesleyan University (www.library.edu/friendex.htm) offers smaller categories and showcases what the friends can offer members: circulation privileges, reference requests and more. At the Willis N. Hackney Library (Barton College) the friends hosts a dinner lectureship twice a year.[12] Friends memberships run from five dollars for students to one thousand dollars for lifetime members. Their speakers have included Clyde Edgerton, Kaye Gibbons, Gail Godwin, and mystery novelist Margaret Maron. While dinner events require considerable effort on the part of volunteers (and staff) to arrange (and no insubstantial expense), they are quite exciting and successful.[13] In small communities, they are just the ticket for creating an atmosphere of excitement and wonder.

KING-SIZED OUTREACHES

At King College, in Bristol, Tennessee, another annual dinner event occurred from 1979–1986. In a town of only 30,000, the Friends of the E. W. King Library brought in the internationally known writers Alex Haley, Michael Novak (Templeton Award winner), the late John Erlichman (of Watergate fame), Kathryn Koob (of Iranian hostage fame) William F. Buckley Jr. (the notable political pundit and reigning conservative intellectual), award-winning Madeleine L'Engle (children's writer) and Arthur Schlesinger Jr. (historian and pundit). In six years, this library with a total volume count of under 100,000 (and total enrollment of under five hundred) grossed over $70,000. The annual event became *the* social occasion of the year.[14]

The Friends of the Medford Public Library organized to support the library as it services the community, promote its particular services, assist in making the library a more user-friendly place and enhance collections and services through fund-raising.[15] At the Friends of the Westport Public Library, support and advocate the library in ways already mentioned. But this group has been around since the 1940s, expanding the library's cultural services through more than two hundred programs, which are free and open to the public.[16] In 2002 the group raised more than $29,000 for the book collection, one thousand five hundred dollars to support book discussion groups, and $20,000 to the library's technology fund. No wonder the picture of the friends president presenting the library board's trustee presidents shows them grinning from ear to ear.

At Bryn Mawr Friends of the Library (www.brynmawr.edu/Library/Docs/fol.html) the friends celebrated the addition of the library's one-millionth volume, "Many [of which] were acquired with funds raised by the Friends…[and] [m]any more…given by individual Friends or through the mediation of Friends." Friends at Bryn Mawr also enjoyed lectures, which covered a wide variety of topics including feminist perspectives on art, architectural history, and the art of the William Morris and Kelmscott presses. The wide variety of the programs assures that eventually something will appeal to a variety of friends members. As we have seen, academic exercises are not mandatory. Variety is the key.

The Friends of the Library of the San Jose Public Library have volunteers, who are "committed to support and supplement needed library resources."[17] The Friends advocate the importance of libraries in the community, raise funds to achieve library goals, and seek out resalable books for the annual book sales. The Web site indicates that friends can "share ideas, time and talents to enrich library services, provide books, cassettes, CDs and magazines for surrounding communities, encourage children to make reading and libraries an essential part of their lives, and enhance technological resources in the library."

The Friends of the Brooklyn College Library (Brooklyn, New York) approach the appeal in the proper vernacular: potential friends know what they are doing for you. That benefit is obvious. What isn't so obvious is what you will do for them. Thus, Brooklyn Friends know up front what they will get.[18] Individual members get borrowing privileges and newsletters from the "Chief Librarian." Each category is cumulative, including all that the rights and privileges that are in lesser categories, plus others. Thus, "dual memberships" get advance notices of exhibits, invitations to Library Week events, and advance notices to the annual booksale. The "Book Collector" memberships get invitations to special Friends events and a copy of the annual report. "Literary Circle" members get personal tours of the New Library. "Conservators" get logo-crested friends memorabilia. "LaGuardia Guild" members get access to database searches, while the final membership level, "Gilded Tower" get special invitations to private homes and a copy of the local historian's latest scribbling. The amounts of the memberships are also creatively contrived, ranging for a low of $50 to a high of $1,000. By making each category cumulative of the preceding ones, high dollar memberships are encouraged.

No one who joins a friends group really expects to get a great deal. Libraries are not, after all, athletic departments or the Junior League. But friends coordinators, if they put their heads and their hearts into the matter, can come up with benefits to proffer that will have great appeal. For example, if famous lectures are held, friends should get first shot at the tickets and at a price that non-friends members cannot take advantage of. A dinner function with, say John Grisham might cost non-friends one hundred dollars a plate, but friends members only fifty dollars. The Brooklyn example of personal searches is particularly creative. Who out there with a child in high school would not jump at the chance to have their own personal reference librarian take their son or daughter on a tour of the literature? Not only is this a real benefit, but it also has the added advantage of showing off the value of libraries and librarians. Of course, it need not be limited to high school term papers. Every librarian knows of dozens of community patrons, who are working either on the great American novel or the next nonfiction best seller. Tax deductible features are also a great advantage.

ME AND MRS. JONES

The G. Eric Jones Friends of the Library has chosen to highlight a particularly bedeviling problem that libraries face annually: budget limitations.[19] "Faced with current budget limitations, the library is looking to its friends for support in maintaining and strengthening its role as a regional cultural institution. You can help." Precisely. Listed are specific goals: library automation, library acquisitions, special collections, repair and restoration of library materials, and more. The friends also offer numerous advantages: campus and community events, fall and spring book sales, bookmarks, postcards, lectures, "keepsakes,"

TIP: Remember this important fund-raising point: *ask for more than you think you will get.*

and more. This group also thinks big. Memberships range from a low of fifty dollars to a high of five thousand. This illustrates another important fund-raising point we will revisit later: *ask for more than you think you will get.*

Some friends groups will give out mugs, pens, pencils, and commemorative Jefferson Cups. Such offerings are more than useful. They highlight a certain event—the King College Friends Group gave out Jefferson Cups commemorating the event, complete with the date and name of the speaker—while keeping the library's name before the benefactor. Imagine having a Jefferson Cup with your library's name on it sitting on the shelf of many of the attendees. Everyday he or she sees it and, what is more, guests to the house also see it and are attracted to it. Fountain or ballpoint pens are also very effective. At the library where I now work, we give out logo-crested pens at every opportunity. My surprise is only matched by my delight when I see these out in the community being used by people I have never met (at least until I see the pen).

L.A. FRIENDS

As one would expect, no one does it any better than the Friends of the Los Angeles Public Libraries. The County of Los Angeles Public Library has seventy-three friends groups with a membership of *nearly six thousand two hundred.*[20] Friends in these groups promote good will for the libraries, educate the public on the needs of libraries, and provide cultural and educational programs throughout. They provide program assistance to public libraries countywide, recruit volunteers to serve in these libraries, raise funds, and advocate library-friendly legislation on behalf of the library. They also encourage all friends groups to join Friends of the Library U.S.A. (FOLUSA), as all good groups should (more about FOLUSA below).

Friends of the Courtright Memorial Library at Otterbein College in Westerville, Ohio, called upon a local professor to design its 2000–2001 bookmark.[21] The design has an illuminated manuscript look. Otterbein has drawn upon faculty and involved them, offered a work of art to would-be friends, and penned a lovely biography for all to read. A very innovative idea is called "Raise a Mile of Pennies." Members are asked to save pennies in rolls and bring the rolls to the library. These are laid end-to-end until they reach a mile. When complete, the "mile of pennies" will total $10,560. This mimics what every citizen can relate to: pennies for highways. The library also produced "Midnight at the Millennium" a murder-mystery play that used local players and was "premiered" at the annual meeting. Doubtless this garnered the applause of all.

The Friends of the Milwaukee Public Library supports the area public libraries and library literacy. Benefit categories include the "Novel," the "Special Edition," the "Bestseller," the "Classic," the "Opus" and the "Masterpiece."[22]

At the Friends of the Robert Manning Strozier Library at Florida State University, one of the many Friends activities is the design and sale of note cards. The cards highlight buildings on the FSU campus (the library, of course, being the most important). Each of the four sets contain twelve buildings and make excellent birthday or hostess gifts, or just a simple treasure for a good friend, relative, or business partner. Because FSU is so large the friends there are able to offer special discounts on the Friends of FSU publishing ventures. These nicely bound books make great gifts or keepsakes. Not every library can do something as ambitious as running its own press, but the idea of manufacturing locally friends-made memorabilia should be remembered.

EXCELLENCE AWARD

The Friends of the Library of Wellesley College offers poetry readings by poets in residence, rare books, artists' books, and more. The help of the Friends of the Library is listed as one of the reasons the Wellesley College Library received the first ever Excellence in Academic Libraries Award (2000), given by the Association of College and Research Libraries (ACRL). Because many friends are retired and are unable to attend the events, the library makes a habit of posting on its Web site pictures of friends events after the fact. The friends have purchased color inject plotter for the Knapp Media and Technology Library, Vandercook proof press, the Books Arts Laboratory, restoration of the Elizabeth Barrett Browning Chair Collections, the Ellesmere Chaucer Manuscript Collections and more. Giving credit, and giving it often, is always a good practice. Having a place on your Web page for the contributions of friends groups is a way of saying thank you, and also encouraging others to do likewise. It is also a way of encouraging even larger gifts, such as the $250,000 gift Wellesley received for book conservation.[23]

Meanwhile, the Lexington Public Friends of the Library formed its group in 1966. As the group matured it offered such exciting programs as "Evenings with Kentucky Authors." None other than Barbara Bush spoke at the friends gathering while her husband was President. The friends group specializes in a colossal book sale each year.[24]

BEEN THERE, CAN'T DO THAT

Some may be saying, "But I can't start a friends group. I've tried but there just isn't any way our [fill in the blank] will allow it." Are you doomed just to read about what other libraries are doing? Not necessarily. Sometime you have to prove the value of a thing before its value is recognized. At Oklahoma Baptist University, the Mabee Learning Center found itself in just about that place: between a rock and hard place. All development activities were tightly controlled and heavily monitored. Starting a friends group proved too problematic. Moreover, the staff of the development office was simply too small to undertake the enterprise on the library's account and still attend the overall needs of the university.

Enterprising librarians there decided to take matters into their own hands, invited a rare book expert out to view their rare book collection (it had been housed in boxes in vacant stairwells and only recently placed in an uncontrolled environment with shelves). After the antiquarian's visit, the librarians wrote up a proposal to dispose of the collection. The end result? More than $100,000 was added to the library's (until then) nonexistent materials endowment in a matter of weeks.

Granted, this is a highly unusual approach and does not exactly fall under the rubric "Friends Activities." But it does give vent to an age-old adage: there's more than one way to skin a cat (with apologies to cat-lovers). With such money in place, future librarians to that facility will be able to draw on that external support and move the library even farther ahead.

FRIEND-RAISING

In the end, the penultimate meaning of friends groups is *Friend-raising*. It is a process wherein a friends group (or library) identifies potential "fellow-travelers" and attempts to bring them together for a common cause: to improve the library in question. Friends groups are for fun, for fellowship, for getting together and talking about books of whatever stripe happens to be their fancy. It doesn't always have to be literary, as we've seen. It can be scientific books, books about social work or social theory, or even about politics. The main thing is to find out what the common thread is and begin to weave that into the warp and woof of the library's tapestry of services. Like Theseus who used a thread to find his way our of the maze, so librarians can use the common thread of friends groups to help find their way out of financial imbroglios, or provide advocates to achieve the same. Any difficult road is made so

> In the end, the penultimate meaning of friends groups is *Friend-raising*.

much the better if traveled with those who share a common purpose, a kindred sentiment. In many ways that is what friend-raising is all about: finding a unifying theme among those who can aid you in a shared task. But that is the *penultimate* purpose.

FRIENDS OF ALL VARIETIES

Friends groups can take almost any form, but the species of the genus generally fall into Advocacy, Volunteerism, and Budgetary Support (both budget-relieving and budget-enhancing). We provide a brief explanation of these three activities here, and go into more detail later in the book. Advocacy groups are very important and can provide budgetary support, but that is not their chief end. Volunteer groups are also extremely important as their efforts promote not only support but also the potential for later financial gain. Furthermore, you can constitute one kind of group that pursues more than one kind of support—indeed, it is recommended. But given the current economic times, I believe there is only one kind that should be vigorously pursued.

The *ultimate* purpose of any friends groups should be about raising money, and not just about raising a handful of dollars. It's about raising *significant* funds. While some readers may contest this statement, for those involved in friends groups there is no question about it. This is not to be dismissive of other types of groups, for example advocacy groups. But unless your library is blessed with too many staff members with too little to do, chances are those working in your library are overworked already. Asking them to do more—and do not be deceived, friends groups require a great deal of work—for a few extra altruistic dollars for the library falls under the heading of cruel and unusual punishment. Too many friends groups begin poorly only to end worse. If you have in mind planning a group that will contribute a few thousand dollars to augment the book budget, you're not only planning too small, but planning in the wrong direction. If you are going to do this at all, do it boldly, and on a grand scale. Quite simply, to justify the time and energy involved, the enterprise will need to produce revenue sufficient to cover far more than basic costs. Experience has shown, however, that unless you pursue your goal energetically, it is unlikely you will achieve it.

Of course, getting one going at all is the first step. At the beginning of this chapter I pointed out how few academic libraries are supported by friends groups. Part of the reason may lie in the workload conditions of those institutions. It appears, however, that any librarian who has the chance of improving her library, and the library's acquisitions with a

> The *ultimate* purpose of any friends groups should be about raising money, and not just about raising a handful of dollars.

friends group, had better be about becoming involved with one, or consider another profession altogether. We have examined the wide variety of friends groups. We've seen just how many varieties are out there, and how many different ways such groups can be configured. We can safely say that the kind of group a librarian has at her command is limited only by her imagination.

Further, we've surveyed the economic conditions of libraries and found them to be like Belshazzar: wanting. Friends groups for librarians fall under the win-win options that life rarely offers. So, there is need, great need, and some would even say critical need. Secondly, there is limitless variety. One cannot complain that there simply isn't a form or a type that appeals. Yet, there may be another reason. Perhaps a librarian is reading this and saying, "Yes, all of that sounds very well and good. What you are telling me is that I'll essentially be flying by the seat of my pants. I haven't time for that. I can't undertake something entirely on my own that requires considerable time and high risk." The reply is, you are only half right.

Friends groups do take time and that time *must* have the undivided attention of the dean or the director of the library. Few groups have any chance at success without a committed dean or director behind them. If his or her commitment cannot be guaranteed, then all the rational advice tells us to steer clear. As to "going this alone" however, nothing could be further from the truth.

YOU'VE (ALREADY) GOT A FRIEND

Yeoman's work has been done for those interested in friends groups by FOLUSA, Friends of the Library U.S.A. FOLUSA contains far many more public libraries in its fold than it does academic ones, but that's not important. Initiating a friends group in a library is pretty much the same, whether that library is an academic one, public, special, or even a high school library. Vast resources are at your command through FOLUSA.[25] There are also colleagues throughout the United States and Europe who are willing to proffer advice.

> Vast resources are at your command through FOLUSA (Friends of the Library U.S.A.).

Not much can be done for those who simply do not want to begin a friends group. But, for those who do, there are many people who would be not only happy to help, but also flattered that you asked. So, what are you waiting for? Certainly there is considerable need. The economic conditions surrounding all libraries could not be more bleak. States are cutting funds everywhere you turn, so no library is "safe" from such budget cuts. Only those ignorant of these conditions, or those who choose to look at the world through rose-colored glasses have missed them. The time is now. The hour is late. All that remains is for you to act.

> ### AT A GLANCE
>
> - Today's economic climate requires an old solution to an old problem.
> - Inflation rates for library materials outstrip even health care increases.
> - Annual budgets never really handled all the library's needs; they just seemed to.
> - While never abundant, friends groups have flourished at both special and public libraries.
> - Academic librarians have been slow to take up the friends clarion call.
> - The variety of friends groups is endless.
> - Even where obstacles impose, a friends group, or something like it, can solve a multitude of budget problems.
> - Any number of friends groups are possible: advocacy, volunteerism, and budgetary.
> - Given today's budgetary climate, budget relieving and/or enhancing appear the best alternatives.
> - Nothing of value comes easy, and starting—and continuing—a friends group is hard work.
> - Friends of the Library U.S.A. (FOLUSA) stands ready to help any new or old group. FOLUSA is the best friend of any librarian hoping to create or revive a friends group.

ENDNOTES

1. As I write this (2003), only two states, New Mexico and Wyoming, have state budgets in the black. For more see T.J. Hennen, Jr., "Performing Triage on Budgets in the Red," *American Libraries* 34, no. 3 (March 2003): 36–38.

2. This is an extrapolated figure. From 1998 to 2000, U.S. periodicals in academic institutions went up forty percent. See "Five Year Journal Price Increase—U.S. Libraries." (1998–2000). Available at www-us.ebsco.com/home/printsubs/history.pdf. For more general information see Ebsco's "Serials Price Projections and Cost History" at www-us.ebsco.com/home/printsubs/priceproj.asp.

3. This is not political commentary. See Joshua Murvachik, *Heaven on Earth: The Rise and Fall of Socialism* (San Francisco. Encounter Books, 2002).

4. The Tennessee situation mentioned above led to the University of Tennessee "manning" its main library with twenty workers instead of the usual one hundred fifty. It proved only temporary but should serve as a wake-up call to everyone who works at a public or private institution. If it can happen there, it can happen anywhere. What is worse, it most likely will happen wherever you work before economic times improve.

5. The "he" here is not sexist. I happen to know the male librarian who began it.

6. See www.simbury.lib.ct.us.friends.htm and www.booksale.org, respectively.

7. See www2.ncsu.edu/ncsu/, under "Friends of the Library."

8. Leland Parks, Winthrop Library Advisory Board meeting, Winthrop University, November 2001.

9. See http://library.tamu.edu/develop/freinds/member.htm.

10. Ibid.

11. See www.mppl.lib.in.us/friendshome.htm.

12. http://library2.barton.edu/libraryinformation/friends.asp.

13. For details on planning such an event see my book, *Organizing Friends Groups* (New York: Neal-Schuman, 1993).

14. I know this to be true because I was involved in its inception.

15. See http://friendsmpl.home.att.net.

16. See www.westportlibrary.org/about/friends/index.html.

17. See www.sjpl.lib.ca.us/About/friends.htm.

18. See http://academic.brooklyn.cuny.edu/library/friends.htm.

19. For more see http://199.232.32.170/screens/libinfo_20html.

20. See http://colapublib.org/support/friends.html.

View this masterful and beautiful bookmark at www.otterbein.edu/resources/library/libpages/Friends/June2000news.htm.

See www.mpl.org.File/found_friends.htm.

23. This is a site well worth the visit and will provide many useful ideas: www.wellesley.edu/Library/friends.html.

24. See www.friendsbookcellar.org/friends/history.html.

25. And not only through FOLUSA. There are also books like this one, as well as numerous others. Of course I'm partial, but my own title, *Organizing Friends Group* in Neal-Schuman's How-to-Do-It series, is also highly recommended, as are all those cited here.

2 GETTING A FRIENDS GROUP STARTED

FRIENDS GROUP—GETTING STARTED

Surely the first chapter has alacrified your curiosity about friends groups. Perhaps you knew for some time that economic conditions *vis-a-vis* your library demanded your attention and redress but were unsure if friends groups were the answer. Now, however, after you've witnessed first hand their endless variety and success, no doubt you are ready to think about beginning a friends group. Do you just start calling people? Not yet.

Before rushing headlong into the open void and risking vertigo you need to understand a few things from the get-go. Some of them may surprise you. Whether you, as head of a given library, have been ordered to begin one, or you are a volunteer who will spearhead the group, this chapter is important. It is vitally important to do intellectual spadework. If you have not thought through what is required to create a friends group, pay close attention; if you have, or think this advice unnecessary, skip to chapter three.

BUILD FOR THE FUTURE

The first bit of advice can be summed up in two words: THINK BIG. Just because you organize one member at a time doesn't mean you should think on a small scale. Have big ideas and big plans, and implement them. It's hard enough to get friends groups going; harder still to keep a *small* friends group trudging on, year after year. I don't mean that you go for big numbers (we'll discuss size later) but for big plans, big funds. In other words, *dream* big. "Another weakness [of friends groups] is for a small group of individuals to carry on from year to year," writes Jack Short.[1] Nothing could be more true. Moreover, such groups tend to have tunnel vision about who they are, or what they are about.

This may be especially true if the new librarian inherits a small, struggling friends group already in place. By small, I mean both in numbers *and in product, or outcome*. While it may sound like heresy,

> Just because you organize one member at a time doesn't mean you should think on a small scale. Have big ideas and big plans, and implement them.

it's better if such groups die on the vine than wither in survival. Too much time and energy is needed to run a group anyway, so it may not be the wisest strategic move to waste the effort on a small, provincial group that will not rise to the occasion of the library's dire needs. The early Christian theologian Origen once wrote, "it's mad idolatry to make service greater than the God." If we apply that to friends groups, it would run, *Remember, it isn't the library that exists for the friends group, but the other way around.*

If you begin by thinking big, you'll doubtless miss it but end somewhere close. If you begin by thinking small, you'll end smaller still. If the current leadership isn't "ready" to tackle larger goals it may be time to get new leadership. That's why the selection of board members who make up the friends group is so important. Their selection is vouchsafed, for good or ill, to begin the group. Jack Short, quoted above, goes so far as to say that weak friends groups must not be tolerated even though those members may be strong library supporters.[2] In other words, it's a good idea to let everyone know early on that this is a group that will *fish*, not cut bait endlessly.

When you think of all the various activities friends groups are responsible for—money, services, money, advocacy, money, public relations, money, community involvement and money—it should be more than obvious that a strong, robust, vital group will be necessary to accomplish even one of those tasks well.[3]

Groups *begin* small. They just cannot *end* there. Karla Kimerer recalls the time she began a public library friends group and started with a few names in a shoebox.[4] But those names quickly added up to eight hundred and about $100,000 in friends funds.[5] Had the shoebox been a permanent fixture, or had those few early names seemed "enough," the highly influential Public Library of Des Moines Foundation would not be in existence. *That's* the spirit one is looking for.

> Groups *begin* small. They just cannot *end* there.

THE LEADER OF THE PACK

That spirit, however, *must* originate with the leader of the group. Now there are several theories or philosophies about who that head, or leader, must be. One school of thought says it can be anyone *except* the director of the library. Another says it can be any volunteer. A third says it *must* be the dean or director of the library. Experience has taught that the third theory is more often than not associated with successful friends groups, but let me clarify that claim.

The first theory takes the approach that the group needs its distance from the library, it needs to be able to make decisions, plan events and host programs without the added vicissitudes of the comings and goings of various directors. This argument has merit, and there are some examples, though not many, of successful friends groups so constituted. Such groups are not wrong but they cannot be successful unless they work very, very closely with the library's head.

The second theory argues from this same angle, but goes one step further to argue that the group needs to be self-supporting, and will be successful regardless of who happens to have its reins in hand at any given time. This, too, has great merit, but there is one fairly large sticking point: it rarely happens. Rarely *does not mean never*, but it does mean not often enough to make it ring convincingly true. In both the first and the second cases, whoever heads up the group must come to know that being the head requires many, many hours of work, all for no pay. What many, though not all, come to realize is that they have to have a *paid* member to run the group between presidents.

The first part of this chapter will try to convince you that the *de facto* leader, whether silent or on the frontlines, *must* be the director, the head librarian, the dean, or whatever title your library has chosen to give its chief librarian. Many will see this statement as controversial so I hope what follows will help to clarify it.

In some ways, it's true that the *day-to-day leader* of the actual group can be anyone. It can be a community member, a member of the faculty (if an academic group), or even a staff member.[6] But the leading light must come from the chief librarian. If he or she is not a central person *from the beginning*, it's unlikely that the friends group will grow beyond a handful of people who like to get together for a few "fun" events, and hand over a few thousand dollars each year. If you think about it, your friends group is (or should be) no different from any other fund-raising outreach. It is generally not run independent of the CEO, or in the library's case, the CIO.

This is important for one simple reason: no one knows better what the library needs than its head, the person in charge. He or she has the vision, has articulated (along with the staff and parent organization) the library's stated mission, and is moving the library forward in the direction that its constituents (i.e., its patrons), have indicated they want it to go. Not to put too fine a point on this, this is the chief librarian's job in the first place. Writing her out of the friends group, or allowing her only an accessory role, is to guarantee a friends group failure. The head librarian shouts the rallying cry, the point-person if you will, who will talk about initiatives, elaborate on goals, explain objectives and call for new equipment, materials or the improvement of facilities. In the end, it is the library head who can effectively *communicate the plan*, whatever it is, and show how to get there. Who knows this better than the head librarian?

> In some ways, It's true that the *day-to-day leader* of the actual group can be anyone... But the leading light must come from the chief librarian.

But it is not just a matter of knowing; it is also a matter of position. Can anyone outside the library, even if he or she is a faculty member, staff member, city council member, the head of the largest industry in the area, know more about the library's mission, or know it better than the library's head? Not only this, but when others must be called upon, whether they are staff in a public library, administrators in an academic setting, or board members from a special library, articulate it better than the library's head?

That's why in Chapter 1, I suggested that if the director, dean, or library head is not on board, it may be better to wait until such time as he or she can be brought on board. But there is another reason as well. If left to their own devices, friends groups without this organizing visionary will turn inward, or worse, turn sour. When groups are left to their own devices, libraries may get the proverbial white elephant—or pink flamingo—and have to figure out what to do with it. If this is not a problem—that is, while you cut half your periodical budget or furlough staff, your friends group presents you with a first edition of the Gutenberg Bible—then there is no reason to continue reading this chapter. On the other hand, if this does strike you as problematic, then you grasp why the dean—or the director or the head of the special library—must be fully on board with the friends group, and on task.

It doesn't matter whether your library is a public, academic, special, or even of the school variety. It does matter that the library's real head is on board, and not merely on board, but involved from the beginning.[7] This cannot be an *ad hoc* role played by the library's "CEO" any more than any other kind of CEO can be "distantly" involved in fund-raising.

In an earlier edition of this book, I said that the chief role does not *necessarily* have to be the library's head.[8] Having worked in friends groups, or with them, for two decades I can say with certainty that I was wrong. In fact, all of us wish it could be otherwise, but you know how those faint hopes go: if wishes were horses beggars would ride. I wish I could tell you that the library head could show up every now and again, give her blessing, leave, and everything would be fine so long as you had a very involved friends group president. I suppose technically that could be construed as correct. The problem is, like socialism, you can never find it working anywhere other than in *theory*. The simple calculus of fund-raising and friends-making does not allow for even a slightly disinterested (or distracted) library head's involvement. He or she *must* be involved, and intimately so. Again, the track record of successful friends groups bears this out.

Earlier I mentioned the different aspects that friends groups accomplish in addition to fund-raising: services, advocacy, public relations, and community involvement. Each of these can be a type or focus of a friends group.[9] But the days of friends groups that have anything other than fund-raising as the *primary* outreach are over, or, in these uncertain economic times for libraries, a waste of time.

WHAT ABOUT 501(C)(3) BYLAWS?

Before going on let me say that this advice is *not* for the rookie library head. If you find a group already in place, you cannot begin from day one making the change. You can, however, over time, begin planting the seed that one day will flower in this fashion. In connection to this, let me add a word about 501(c)3 bylaws. In the first place, the friends group must be incorporated as a nonprofit, a process that takes about three days and will cost about one hundred fifty dollars. The pertinent part of the tax code reads,

> To be tax-exempt as an organization described in the IRC Section 501(c)(3) of the code, an organization must be organized and operated exclusively for one or more purposes set forth in the IRC Section 501(c)(3) and none of the earnings of the organization may inure to any private shareholder or individual. In addition, it may not attempt to influence legislation as a substantial part of its activities and it may not participate in campaign activity for or against candidates.

If your group is governed by a board you have no reason to fear employing the dean or director as more than a figurehead. Besides, most friends groups will more likely be in violation of the last sentence in the above paragraph than any other part of the rule. The code goes on to say that in addition to not being designed for private interests, the earning cannot accrue to one individual, nor can the organization be engaged in transactions that benefit one person, or, *"with a person having substantial influence over the organization."* In which case, if found to be true, an excise tax may be levied. What I am recommending here is not autocratic control, but more than a passing interest by the dean or director.

If the dean or director is merely "present" in the organization, experience has taught that the friends group will never be more than modestly successful, if at all. By design, the governance structure indicates that the executive board must be the proverbial head and this is true. But the dean or director as nothing more than liaison, as one who cannot orchestrate the group in its proper direction, will never go very far.

When you give to your chosen benevolent organizations, do you like to give to the door-to-door collector, a liaison, or the organization's leader? When you ask questions, do you want to hear, "Let me get back to you"? or are you ready for an answer, *now*? Only the library's head can do these things. The library's head must be there to answer questions, name goals, specify where the funds will go and, more importantly, why they are needed. He or she must be there to ask for the gift on many occasions, and that gift must always be *more than what you think your giver can give.*[10] No one can really do these tasks effectively other than the person who holds the reins of the library.

Yet there are more reasons why the library's putative head must be involved to the extent that he or she is the *de facto* head of the friends groups, at least six more.[11] Because life is made up of more than just positive outcomes, these may appear as negative ones. To the squeamish among us, apologies are proffered in surfeit. Nevertheless, they must be addressed.

> **Seven Simple "Don'ts" of Friends Groups:**
>
> - Don't become an exclusive or elitist club;
> - Don't exist without professional development, influence, and control;
> - Don't buy only books for the library (or any other one-item group);
> - Don't let the friends group run themselves or let a librarian who is not the library's head work exclusively with them;
> - Don't present esoteric topics as programs;
> - Don't seek always larger memberships for their own sake;
> - Don't let the friends group become the library's *only* external fund-raising venture.

SEVEN SIMPLE DON'TS OF FRIENDS GROUPS

The library head must be at least the *de facto* head because he or she must see to it that the friends group adheres to the following "don'ts":

1. Don't become an exclusive or elitist club;
2. Don't exist without professional development, influence, and control;
3. Don't buy only books for the library (or any other one-item group);
4. Don't let the friends group run themselves or let a librarian who is not the library's head work exclusively with them;
5. Don't present esoteric topics as programs;
6. Don't seek always larger memberships for their own sake;
7. Don't let the friends group become the library's *only* external fund-raising venture.

Let's examine these in some detail.

Don't become an exclusive or elitist club. Friends groups rarely become exclusive by design; rather, it's by default. After all, they asked everyone *they* know, and all their friends really like what they like. Before long, others who might want to join in the group may feel that the group is unwelcoming, or is pursing goals that have little or no interest for them. Furthermore, extremely small friends groups, believe it or not, can become politically charged or motivated. Not political in terms of national parties necessarily (though some do), but in terms of local campus or community politics. Having become so, all other parties are, for all practical purposes, excluded.

Don't exist without professional development, influence, and control. Perhaps more than any of the others, this may be the single biggest drawback of not having the library head as *de facto* leader. Some groups become quite resistant to advice, change, help, or even improvement. University relations offices, or public library development offices, are staffed with professionals who have some form of training, either at the university or professional level. They know who to contact and how. They know how to "close the deal." Most importantly, they also know who has been asked already and why. Without this ongoing coordination, friends groups may approach a donor who has already been tapped for another project, especially if the friends group is attached to an academic library (this is less true with public libraries). The end result may be that he or she gives nothing to either, or much less than he could.

Don't buy only books for the library (or any other one-item group). When most people see this prohibition they have a natural inclination to want to protest. And the protest would be legitimate if libraries were *only* about books. Does anyone who works in a library believe this to be true? Forget for the moment that this is the twenty-first century. Have libraries, save perhaps for their very early formation, *ever* been about books alone? Now toss that back into the twenty-first century. With bits, bytes, books and more, how is it possible that any friends groups could be allowed to do so little? Additionally, when single-goal friends groups are allowed to exist as such, the upshot is often low-flying aspirations. After all, with more than fifty thousand academic titles—not to mention mass market and trade titles—being published *every* year, how could *any* group ever do more than add a few?

Don't let the friends group run themselves or let a librarian who is not the library's head work exclusively with them. There is only one thing worse than not having the library's head play a more pivotal role than simply as a liaison, and that is to have another librarian, who is not the head, who plays the ersatz lead. This is not about power but about roles. The librarian who is not the head cannot possibly stand in the place of the library head and so cannot do any of the things the library head would normally do. He cannot set policy, cannot state goals, cannot provide leadership and cannot articulate the library's future. When it comes to one goal over another, when it comes to prioritizing those goals, when it comes to saying which of the main concerns will take precedence *this* year, only the library's leader will do.

Moreover, *only the library's leader should do this*. (Remember, it is after all, his or her job.) Anyone else in this role will have to divide his or her time between the friends activities and the job he or she was hired to do.

Don't present esoteric topics as programs. When groups are left alone, they tend to be overly small, consequently seek small gifts, and look for easy, quickly reachable goals. They also know that programs are a good thing to have so they put on programs that appeal primarily to themselves. This is where the library leader makes the necessary tough decisions. Friends groups in a public library rarely fall victim to this temptation, because the "public" of an entire community is made up of so many different individuals. But friends groups in an academic setting may see the "academic" part of who they are as so much larger than it should be. One esoteric program a year may be fine; more than one is sure to run off would-be members.

Don't seek always larger memberships for their own sake. Throughout this chapter and in part of Chapter 1, I have discussed "small" groups quite a bit. Now comes this warning. Isn't there a contradiction here? Not really. This warning is for those who seek only large crowds for their own sake. Groups that move in this direction make the opposite mistake of the previous one that seeks small memberships for the sake of being intimate. If groups that gravitate to the esoteric are wrong, so are groups that pander after the populace for the sake of big numbers. Recently our local paper carried a story about a group that sponsored walkathons. As it turns out, while the group raised a total of nearly $400,000, the money going to the charity (a local hospital) realized *only $15,000*, less than 5% of the total. Fund-raising efforts of this group are likely over compromised, or at the very least, greatly compromised. The same is true for friends groups that seek only larger and larger numbers.

One other word in this regard concerns the myth of a broad base of donors.[12] This myth resides in the misapprehension that support is chiefly made up of numerous small gifts from many donors. While it's true that each friends group will have more smaller-gift-giving members than givers of large ones, it is no less true that the larger gifts are the lion's share of the giving. Friends groups cannot exist on twenty-five or fifty dollar contributions from a few hundred members.

Don't let the friends group become the library's *only* external fund-raising venture. When friends groups are the only fund-raising outreach by the library, it is not just the library that loses. Fund-raising does, too. All the energies are focused on one way of reaching prospects and the upshot is that only one type of giver is identified. The others who exist may not be simply left untapped, *but left untapped by the library*. Another funds-seeking organization or outreach will reach them, but the library will miss out having put all of its fund-raising eggs into the friends basket.

This mistake is so common it has almost become a principle: if the library has a friends group it cannot have any other fund-raising mechanism. But nothing could be further from the truth. Grants, bequests, wills, and one-time gifts should be sought, *pari passu*. To fail to do so is to fail to understand the concept behind both friends-raising and fund-raising.

> **Fund-raising "do's":**
> - Get out of the office
> - Meet people
> - Attend luncheons
> - Shake hands
> - Repeat the same message to every kind of group there is in your community

BUT CAN I DO THIS?

Some who read these words are likely thinking, "That's just not me. I don't like asking for money. It's a shameless task and I simply cannot do it."[13] This is akin to a physician saying, "It's blood, and the sight of it, that makes me ill," or, "I've never really liked being around sick people." Directing a library in the twenty-first century means raising funds. It means that, or it means watching all your grand plans remain such, but on paper alone. Fund-raising *does* mean getting out of the office, meeting people, attending luncheons, shaking hands, and saying the same things over and over again to every kind of group there is in your community. Over the years I have found this an increasingly enjoyable task. Even asking for funds—closing the deal if you will—is no longer a chore. So long as you can divorce yourself from the inevitable negative answer and not take rejection *personally*, asking for funds can also be exciting. Furthermore, nothing *is* more exciting and enervating than asking for that gift and receiving it, again inevitably, if you do your homework well. What could be more gratifying than going back to the office and announcing that project X, which no one thought would ever become a reality, will commence next week?

So tackle the challenge for what it is: an opportunity for your library to grow. Yes, Murphy's Law is at work here, too: it *will* take all the time you have and more. It will interfere with other less glamorous, but no less important tasks. It will be frustrating and, at times, even overwhelming. Anything worth doing carries with it the same earmarks of significant toil. It is also exhilarating like nothing else you'll ever do in library work.

The question comes down to this, as the commercial has it: have you got it in you? Here is proof to the pudding of all those times, in meetings with staff, in discussions with colleagues, in *tête-à-têtes* with your president or board of directors: were all those just words, just things you said, or do you really believe them? If so, you'll take up the challenge of fund-raising via a friends group for the opportunity it is.

AT A GLANCE

- If you think you're ready to go, take a moment to reflect on the cost.
- THINK BIG. All groups begin small, but thinking small only keeps them that way.
- There are several philosophies regarding the role of the dean or director in a friends group.
    - One philosophy argues that the dean/director must not be visible.
    - Another philosopy argues that because the friends group is a dynamic, free-floating support group, anyone should be able to lead it.
    - A final philosophy argues that the dean/director should be more than a mere figurehead.
- All of the philosophies regarding the role of the dean or director have merit, but experience teaches that the third philosophy, in which the dean/director acts as more than a figurehead, has the greatest success.
- While controversial to some, the third philosophy concerning the dean/director's involvement does not conflict with 501(c)(3) rulings.
- The dean/director is no tyrant, but neither is he or she invisible or only an accessory.
- Common sense makes this plain: when you give to a charitable organization or worthy cause, do you like giving to just anyone, or do you like to give to the organization head?
- Friends groups must follow the Seven Simple Don'ts:
    1. Don't become an exclusive or elitist club;
    2. Don't exist without professional development, influence, and control;
    3. Don't buy only books for the library (or any other one-item group);
    4. Don't let the friends group run themselves or let a librarian who is not the library's head work exclusively with them;
    5. Don't present esoteric topics as programs;
    6. Don't seek always larger memberships for their own sake;

> 7. Don't let the friends group become the library's only external fund-raising venture.
>
> • You can do this!

ENDNOTES

1. J. Short, *Library Friends Guidelines* (Avon, CT: Consultant Publications, 1997), 1.
2. Ibid.
3. S. Dolinick, "What Are Friends For?" in *Friends of the Library Sourcebook*, 3rd ed (Chicago: American Library Association, 1996), 1–2.
4. A.R. Albanese, "Foundations for the Future," *Library Journal* 127, no. 8 (May 1, 2002): 40.
5. Ibid. The group now raises about $350,000 annually.
6. M.Y. Herring, *Organizing Friends Groups* (New York: Neal-Schuman, 1993), 4.
7. Obviously, if a new librarian comes into town, and the group is already thriving, it should be part of the interview process to make sure who is hired will be on board from the beginning.
8. Ibid., 9.
9. Indeed, I said as much in *Organizing Friends Groups*, 5–8.
10. See J. Short, above. Also, see V. Steele and S.D. Elder, *Becoming a Fundraiser: The Principles and Practice of Library Development*, 2nd ed. (Chicago: American Library Association, 2000), 5.
11. Because I cannot state them any better myself, and see no reason to reinvent the wheel, I cite Steele and Elder above. I have rearranged the order and changed some of the language to serve my purposes here but the points are those of Steele and Elder.
12. K.S. Kelley, *Fundraising and Public Relations: A Critical Analysis* (Hillsdale, NJ: Lawrence Erlbaum Associates, 1991), 140.
13. For wonderful instruction on these and other points, read Kelley, ibid., and her equally informative *Effective Fund-Raising Management* (Hillsdale, NJ: Lawrence Erlbaum Associates, 1998). Both are filled with excellent advice and counsel, and not just for the professional development fund-raiser, either.

3 ESTABLISHING THE FRIENDS EXECUTIVE BOARD

THE FRIENDS EXECUTIVE BOARD

If the friends coordinator is one of the most important (if not *the* most important) figure in the friends calculus, then the friends executive board is by far the single most important group. If you have never been involved in a friends group, or are trying to set one up, start by establishing a steering committee. I wrote at length about this in the first edition of *Organizing Friends Groups* and will not rehash it now. Suffice it to say that the steering committee acts as your start-up board. Individuals chosen to serve on that board *may* later become members of your friends executive board, but it is neither mandatory nor always desirable.

Charitable organizations, of which friends groups are but one, must have at least the following four strengths[1]. As a consequence, you'll want to look for friends executive board members who:

- Utilize strategic resources to get gifts;
- Think of alternative sources for the needed gifts;
- Possess the ability to persuade the donor;
- Can help the board survive without the gift.

A short summary will bring these into clearer focus.

STRATEGIC RESOURCES

Friends groups must have money to make money. This is an old but true adage that is often overlooked. This may seem obvious but it is surprising how many friends groups are reluctant, even allergic, to spending a few dollars on the group's identity. Whether it's dollars on the newsletter, or dollars on marketing (about which more, later), some groups simply refuse to spend any money at all other than for the primary cause (which should be plural, not singular), whatever that happens to be. Apparently a vow of poverty is what some friends groups think looks best when asking for funds. A simple test proves the futility of this thinking.

Strengths of a good executive board member:

- Utilizes strategic resources to get gifts
- Thinks of alternative sources for the needed gifts
- Possesses the ability to persuade the donor
- Can help the board survive without the gift

If you receive in the mail a poorly typed, grossly misspelled appeal for funds, or one that is well-reasoned, thoughtful and eye-appealing, which are you likely to respond to favorably? Or take a simpler example. When the doorbell rings, are you more or less likely to open it to a man in a suit or a man with body piercings and tattoos? Granted, in a few years, it will be a man in a suit *with* tattoos and piercings, but for now my meaning is clear. We tend to judge books by their covers, even librarians, and while we may feel it is wrong, ill-mannered and host of other bad things, it is also very much a part of human nature. The same is true for friends groups. Strategic resources *must* be set aside to solicit funds and the steering group is the group that makes that happen. Without these funds, the group may be stillborn.

ALTERNATIVE RESOURCES

Groups cannot long exist with only one donor whose response makes or breaks the group's success. Nor can one person, or even a small group of people, hold the key to the success of even *one* friends' goal. A number of individuals should be held in mind for various and particular purposes and goals. Only then can the friends group have any hope of both short- and long-term success. Again, it is the friends executive board that holds the key to this future. They will know, or should, persons who have (or persons who know others who have) the ability to identify help on a particular project. Without such people on board, and willing to make your projects happen, the friends group may not fail, but it will certainly never fly very high.

> A number of individuals should be held in mind for various and particular purposes and goals.... Again, it is the friends executive board that holds the key to this future.

ABILITY TO PERSUADE THE DONOR OR DONORS

No one person, even one who has lived in the community for thirty or more years, is going to know everyone. Enter the friends executive board. The board should know, individually or collectively, those in the community to call on for fund-raising purposes. If they do not know them personally they should know others who do. Their chief function, however, is in the ability to introduce the friends group to those it needs to cultivate.

By using their leverage, collectively or individually, friends executive board members are able to persuade, convince, or otherwise explain why joining the friends group is important. Without these key individuals who not only *can* do this, but who also *will* do this, the friends group will struggle in its efforts to raise funds. Note the "who will" phrase. Friends members can be a peculiar lot, and some may be on the board simply to be on a board. The key is finding influential, *active* members.

An old fund-raising saw runs something like this: money talks to money, or wealth speaks to wealth. Although truisms can be tired and annoying, we often forget one important point: they are generally true. To have the ability to get to donors requires a number of things, not the least of which is to know which donor or donors to contact. Often this comes with social standing. Again the importance of having on the friends executive board individuals who can "connect the [social] dots" is instrumental to having a successful friends group.

SURVIVABILITY WITHOUT THE GIFT

Finally, it is essential that groups be able to survive without any single donor or his or her gift. Each group has to be able to function on its own without having to rely on the local "Daddy Warbucks" to see them through. Often, small philanthropic groups find themselves in this predicament, and not a few friends groups do as well. Why this is true will become apparent momentarily. For now the one word "autonomy" will suffice to explain this principle's purpose.

TIP: Don't place all your eggs in one basket. Make sure your funding comes from various sources.

Friends groups must be able to "walk away" from some donors or gifts in order to make certain the group is free to function as it likes. If all of one's collective eggs are placed in one basket, it becomes increasingly important that the basket remain undisturbed. If a slight movement one way of the other can upset the project or the *raison d'être* of the friends group, then it is likely that the group will fall either to the tyranny or the ecstasy of one donor's thinking. Unfortunately, it is more often the former than the later.

Now that we know the principles behind the friends executive board, it should prove easier to go about choosing the members themselves. While not *every* member will be chosen from outside the ranks of the library's setting, many will be. Choosing them with the idea in mind that they must serve to perpetuate the library's goals goes without saying. It's important to remember, too, that the process of the friends group revolves around *shared decision making*.

It is very easy for two or three individuals to form an unofficial ruling body. After all, they are the only ones who "get things done," or who "are willing to go the distance." What happens in such groups is, though no one means for it to happen, everyone else believes the lie: they are not needed because two or three members have already decided the matter. All other opinions are unnecessary. All of which points to the importance of choosing people of a certain bent to be on your executive board. If this is the first such board, their choice is critical because they will likely choose and/or suggest their successors. Taking time to choose wisely and well will reap rich benefits. Here is the prototype of the perfect executive board member: she works well in groups; she gets things done; she welcomes challenging work; and she doesn't know the meaning of failure. Let's look at these.

Likes working in groups. Such people do not mind sharing the glory. They look out for each other. They give full ventilation to various ideas, but are also eager to get down to work. While they like to work in groups, they are not individuals who will prolong a matter simply to avoid coming to a conclusion. It is important to remember that these individuals will represent the library. Choose them as ambassadors who will represent you well, not those whom you'll have to "call home" for ineffectiveness.[2]

Likes getting things done. It stands to reason that people who will be willing to work in such a context are already successful. But don't make the mistake that success in one thing equals success in another. Choose according to their overall accomplishments. Some potential candidates *may* be resumé builders, nothing more. Look at the track record and see if it matches what you need. The second part of getting things done is they do not want to talk a matter to death, thus eliminating some academics. Of course that is painting with a broad brush, and we do not want to fall victim to a stereotype. But stereotypes come to be so for important truths they reveal, however minor. The fact of the matter is that a fair number of academics really *dislike* coming to a conclusion. They would much rather report "tentative findings."

Is not afraid of work. Members of the friends executive board should be chosen for their willingness to *work*. It will not help matters if you have three very vigorous members but the fourth is a severe stumbling block. Such a friends executive board member will merely steer the friends group into a dead end, or worse. They have to see the goals, operationalize them, and then go after them. For example, if a given friends executive board member knows a dozen possibly helpful individuals but will not contact even one, even a relative, on the library's behalf, what has your group gained?

Does not know the meaning of failure. When beginning a friends group it is quite natural to begin looking in areas one knows best. Such places may not always be the best places to begin, or even end. A considerable number of individuals "like the library." In fact, like mom and apple pie, it is difficult to find anyone who routinely criticizes libraries.[3] On the other hand, when it is time to roll up the sleeves and go after funds, that kind of person may not be the kind of person one wants at all.

Now that you know the *type* of individual you want, it is time to begin finding those individuals. A good beginning place is within your community's civic clubs, especially if your friends group is attached to a public or special library. A quick check of the Chamber of Commerce's Web site will doubtless help you find all of these groups.

The perfect executive board member

- Works well in groups
- Gets things done
- Welcomes challenging work
- Doesn't know the meaning of failure

ESTABLISHING THE FRIENDS EXECUTIVE BOARD   33

It is not a bad idea to talk with their leaders. Let them know what you have in mind and why you want to do it. It may spark interest right away.

If the friends builder is in an academic setting, checking with the college or university's relations outreach is an excellent place to begin. Chances are, some departments (or colleges if at a university) already have advisory boards or friends executive boards. Talk to those leaders. Above all, work with the development office to identify potential friends executive board members.

All of this takes time, of course. There will be lunches and dinners to attend and hands to shake. There will be meetings before work and meetings after hours. There's no getting around this and the friends organizer simply must plan on this from the beginning. The friends builder or coordinator will have to put in numerous volunteer hours to make this happen. Working with the library's head will help lessen the amount of time. Making these rounds serves a number of good purposes. First, it identifies the need. Second, it associates the friends leader with the group that is being formed. Third, it allows that leader to begin an address file that can be used later.

Once you have gone through this process it will be time to begin asking individuals. It is important to point out to them what you expect of them. The following is by no means exhaustive, but it serves as a good starting point for the cultivation of the friends executive board.

Friends executive board members should be expected do all these things and it should be spelled out in your bylaws that this is what you expect. You could subsume these points in your bylaws as: to support the library financially, draw support to the library, attend friends meetings, and recruit other members.

> Executive board members should be expected to support the library financially, draw support to the library, attend friends meetings, and recruit other members.

Support the library financially. This is obvious, or rather it should be, but many who begin a group fail to realize its significance. Friends executive board members should provide, as they are able financially, *leadership* giving. Remember that *the sum of your gifts is in direct proportion both to those you ask and the amount for which you ask*. If you never ask for the gift, chances are you will not get it.[4] So, ask the right members to be on your friends executive board, then ask for the right gift. It is not necessary to ask the very day you ask them to join the board. You must make very clear, however, that a gift is expected of them at some near future date.

Draw support to the library. This is easily as important as the individual financial support you expect of each board member. Each member of the friends executive board should be ready, willing and able to recruit others to the board. They must be willing to call upon others, solicit their help (even in gift giving), and suggest others whom, they know, or can introduce you to those who know them.

Attend friends meetings. This may seem like one of those statements to which the anticipated response, in the common vernacular, would be "Duh!" Unfortunately, you would be surprised how many will undertake the challenge and then never attend even *one* meeting. The effect of this is demoralizing on many within the organization. Imagine putting together a friends executive board and have one-third of the members show up at meetings, and always the *same* one-third. Of course a given meeting may conflict with other meetings your members must attend. If they are the right people—effective, energetic, goal oriented—then you will doubtless run into conflict every now and again. That is why it is always a good a idea to give your members ample warning of upcoming meetings, even as much as thirty days in advance.

Schedule your meetings with the idea in mind that you can overcommit even the most ardent library devotee. Two to four board meetings a year is hardly excessive. On the other hand, twelve to twenty-four may scare off everyone.

Recruit other members. One of the most important functions of these board members is the ability they have to suggest names of *other* board members. If you structure your bylaws carefully (see the Friends Group Starter Kit, part A) board members will be serving three year terms at most. Since recruitment is an annual affair, at any given time, once the board is up and running, members will rotate off. If you do not require this as part of the board member's responsibility, at the end of the first three years, you will be holding meetings to empty rooms.

This begs the question that during the first three years of your operation, you will want to stagger the terms of service so your whole board will no rotate off during the same calendar year. This means that some individuals will serve *more* than three years. It really cannot be helped. Anyone who is willing to serve will be agreeable to this arrangement.

THAT FIRST MEETING

The group is in place and now a meeting must be called. Your executive board member calls it and then asks you to lead it. What do you do? First of all, try to schedule an evening meeting and provide a meal. If you are concerned that you will be spending too much money, then provide ample hors d'oeuvres. This not only solves the problem of when to schedule the meeting (if without dinner, it should be no later than six o'clock), but also provides a nice segue into the business portion of the meeting.

Items that will likely be included during a meeting—whether the dean/director or executive board president leads it—should include the following: where you are now, where you want to be, new accomplishments, special problems (optional) and grants and/or foundation support.

> **Important meeting agenda items:**
> - where you are now
> - where you want to be
> - new accomplishments
> - special problems
> - grants and/or foundation support

Where you are now. A brief review of any existing problems and special circumstances is always helpful to board members. If the executive board president leads the meeting the director can supply her with the needed information. It may well be that there will be a "librarian's report" and this would be the time to focus on these issues. It is also a great time to point out to members much that they do not know about library operations. Not technical matters, of course, but financial ones. I have yet to point out to a board that academic libraries pay three or four times as much for periodicals as individual subscribers and not have at least ninety percent of the audience gasp in disbelief. Visual aids are also very effective. At one Web site, you discover that you can buy either a database, or a new Saturn automobile.[5] The important point is that you share something with your board that helps them understand better both your job and their job. It should not—must not—become lost in a morass of technical libraryese.

Where you want to be. PowerPoint presentations work *if used well*.[6] Just be sure that these are not the *only* presentation, but are *aids* to expressing yourself. Of course PowerPoint isn't the *only* way, but it is a good way of conveying a large amount of information in a short amount of time.[7] Charts, graphs, and goals statements are also useful to share with members. Because most presentation software has the feature of printing usable handouts, board members will leave with a ready-made memory.

Varying the meeting format is another good way to keep members informed, while piquing their interests. One way to do this is to call upon local speakers to address problems. For example, there may be a librarian in a neighboring state or town, far enough away where you would not be competing for the same friends-raising pool, yet close enough to keep expenses down. She could come and talk with your board members about the fund-raising process there. Another individual who is very effective at fund raising in general could come and talk with your group, with adaptations for the library setting. As time goes on, specific goals will be addressed and the group's progress on those goals relayed. A beginning meeting might talk about why these particular goals were chosen in the first place, and why they are needed.

New accomplishments. Every meeting ought to have something good to report. Although your particular situation may be bleak, it is important that board members know the honest truth, of course, but also some good honest successes. This can be hard for the weary librarian who is everyday greeted with yet more reasons to cancel this title or discontinue that standing order for budgetary reasons. But if you remember that your board does not know the library all that well, and will view very differently each success you report, you should have something positive to share at each meeting. Some of this you will have done already when you recruited each member. Once they are on board, they will need some elaboration. Perhaps yours is the only public library that has a certain offering, the only special library in the city, state or region, or the largest undergraduate facility in your area. Whatever it is, you have got to find that upbeat message and exploit it. You cannot give the impression that your hand is eternally frozen in the open position, and that your library's singular claim to fame is your grossly underfunded status. Included here are also the new accomplishments of the group. Every executive board meeting should include some positive things the group has accomplished—new money it has raised, special gifts, and, above all, new purchases. The dean/director may be called upon to elaborate on how effective these purchases are.

Other accomplishments can be publications by library staff, special awards, civic contributions and the like. A short "staff minute" can also be used effectively. What you must resist is a program that drags members through each library department and tries to make each one of them an ad hoc librarian. The idea is to whet the appetite, not satiate forever any desire ever to know more. Odd as it is to write, not everyone views libraries, or their importance, the way we librarians do.

Special problems. One must be careful about how one addresses special problems, because the idea is to inform not to depress. But every group will have its ups and downs and the executive board needs to know when things are not going well. The group may be having fund-raising difficulties (I should say *will* have) and so here is a good place to talk about them. It is important that members know goals are critical to your success, and that the creation of the friends group is not merely to have programs but to raise money to address needs.

The library may be facing a critical shortage of some kind and by presenting it, the friends can undertake it as a special fund-raising event. Do not allow reporting in either case to brand the group or the library as the region's loser. All groups and libraries have problems, the key is presenting them as challenges.

Bear in mind that special problems must be ones that the friends group can address. For example, needing to hire a new staff members is not really the bailiwick of the friends group. Ditto that for low salaries, or inadequate library staff development funds.[8] Both are budget items that most people expect to be part of the ongoing support for the library. On the other hand, special one-time equipment needs, endowment funds for specified items, and, of course, building funds are all the kinds of needs that any donor would consider legitimate "fair game" for a development campaign. Obviously, the attainment of any goal, however small, provides great reportage to members at the next event, or featured in the next newsletter.

Grants and/or foundation support. Many friends groups will begin well, but end poorly, often because the group is the only fund-raising mechanism in the library. One way the friends group can avoid

> Every executive board meeting should include some positive things the group has accomplished—new money it has raised, special gifts, and, above all, new purchases.

this is by bringing in extra funds through foundation support and grants. Friends coordinators will need to work with the larger development arm of the organization. (If necessary, break this activity off from the friends and make it a second fund-raising arm.) Apart from helping to achieve some larger goals, this is important because it also provides the friends with empirical evidence that the library is serious about raising external funds. Besides, friendly competition is always healthy. If the library staff can help, friends members will not feel that they are the only ones working at the fund-raising task. If the library stresses this need, and then does little to help itself toward its fulfillment, special pleas will ring hollow over time.

At the very first executive board meeting, the president should also form subcommittees and solicit volunteers. Subcommittees such as the program committee, new member committee, special projects committee, publicity committee, and the like are some of the many that could be named. All are important, but the solicitation of new members may be one of the most for obvious reasons. The publicity will be vital in seeking to make known the group and its value. It will also undertake a newsletter, whether electronic, in paper, or both. Securing someone with good writing skills is critical. (The chapter on publicity will spell out this and other matters in more detail.)

FRIENDS GROUPS HELP THOSE WHO HELP THEMSELVES

It should go without saying that *every* library staff member, whether professional or not, should be involved financially with the friends. Even if they join at the lowest possible level, it is still critically important that every library employee be involved. One cannot make this mandatory, but repeated emphasis on this point should be sufficient. Convincing staff of the importance of joining the cause is critically important. Moreover, it also helps in gaining foundation and grant support when one can point to one hundred percent participation of staff.

EXERCISING YOUR FRIENDS MUSCLES

A strong, involved friends executive board can make or break a friends group. Identifying the right people takes time and energy. But once found, the right men and women in the friends executive board will bring long and continued success to any friends group. While a robust friends executive board will help any friends group endure over time, it

> A strong, involved friends executive board can make or break a friends group. Identifying the right people takes time and energy. But once found, the right men and women in the friends executive board will bring long and continued success to any friends group.

should be quite obvious that finding the right people is critical to a newly formed one. Because success in such groups is often slow and requires patience, a strong friends executive board will take such groups through the early vicissitudes common to them, and help the group experience success.

Drawing from business resources, the friends executive board, also can provide leadership is assessing need, planning, communication, and implementation, as well.[9] Because it is likely that at least one other library person other than the director or dean will serve on this committee, these roles are also appropriate. Besides providing excellent service in assessment, it will also provide the committee with an assignment and a deadline—two very critical points we will return to in later chapters. Your group's bylaws (see the Friends Group Starter Kit, part A) will establish the power and reach of this committee. But it is important at the outset not to exclude anything from the committee's bailiwick that may prove helpful to the group later on. Once you have established what the committee will and will not do, it is hard to go back later and add additional duties to what is primarily a volunteer service group. It is better to curtail these duties than try to add them later.

For example, assessment of need could include information provided by the library to the friends executive board that indicates why it is important as a fund-raising need. By having the board disperse this information, it does not then appear as if you are always saying what is needed and what is not. You have an additional voice. Moreover, once the need is met, the committee can come back and ballyhoo the success. Another group of roles might be what Beverly Kaye calls the seven Cs, though for our purposes, they are only three in number: clout, conviction and closure.[10] Clout has to do with the ability to attract the right people. Conviction has to do with being "sold" on the library. Closure, however, may be the most important. All too often friends groups do not bring closure to various tasks. The effect is that the group never accomplishes anything while always adding more. When goals are met, or must be abandoned, state it clearly so all will know.

Finally, it is important to remember that the overall goal of any friends executive board is "to provide guidance and direction for planning."[11] The group can help establish purpose and principles, define the boundaries of the outreach, delineate the importance of the work, identify key players, and lay the groundwork for leadership and implementation.[12]

After examining this lengthy list it may appear to some that a given community may not have these kinds of individuals. This is rarely if ever the case. Every community has all of the right players to create a successful Friends group. It is the dean's or director's job to find them and link them up with others. Clearly choosing the *right* players is important. Failure to do so will weaken the committee and therefore

> Every community has all of the right players to create a successful Friends group. It is the dean's or director's job to find them and link them to the group.

weaken the overall effectiveness of the committee *and* the friends groups. By now it should be rather obvious that this is not something that can be undertaken quickly or without deliberation. Moreover, it may not be the people who want to serve, who volunteer themselves, are the best people to ask. A library head who is new to the community and who does not already have a friends group in place, will have to take on this process very slowly, gather information, and the act on her best knowledge of the needs and the people at hand. While such groups should represent the community, member should not be chosen based on anything other than ability and willingness to serve.

AT A GLANCE

- Good friends executive board member should:
    - Utilize strategic resources to get gifts;
    - Think of alternative sources for the needed gifts;
    - Possess the ability to persuade the donor;
    - Help the board survive without the gift.
- The prototypical board member works well in groups, gets things done, welcomes challenging work, and doesn't know the meaning of failure.
- Look for would-be executive members in civic groups and other nonprofit outreaches. Draw from your own knowledge and from the knowledge of your staff and acquaintances.
- Glad-handing is all part of the process, so get used to it.
- Each board member must support the friends financially, draw support to the library, either financial or in-kind, attend board meetings and recruit others to the board.
- Friends executive board meetings have common elements in the agenda that can be tailored to more specific needs:
    - where you are now
    - where you want to be
    - new accomplishments
    - special problems
    - grants and/or foundation support

> • Finally, good board members bring the three Cs to the task: clout, conviction and closure. The use their reputations for the group's advancement, they are "sold" on the library, and they are ready to "close the deal" whenever appropriate.

ENDNOTES

1. K.S. Kelley, *Fundraising and Public Relations: A Critical Analysis* (Hillsdale, NJ: Lawrence Erlbaum Associates, 1991), 209, adapted for this use.
2. This is especially important in academic setting where inquiring minds might just want to inquire instead of know.
3. That is, until libraries took the untoward position of unfettered access to the Internet, and so to the heinousness of the Web's pornography. This is, of course, an entirely different matter but friends-builders need to know that this is a very explosive issue, especially for public libraries. To think it has nothing to do with building a friends group is whistling in the dark.
4. Kelley makes this point, *sic* passim.
5. See www.library.fau.edu/depts/ref/infocost.htm. This site has an enormously useful value in putting things precisely this way. (Many thanks to Vernell Ward at Oklahoma Baptist University, who helped me locate the address I had managed to misplace.)
6. Many such articles warning about the bad uses of PowerPoint can be found using Google or any other search engine. Here's one: www.medicine.uiowa.edu/mstp/students/ppttips.htm.
7. For example, there is the software, Astound, sometimes called "Slides on steroids," that is much more powerful, more capable and just about as easy to use.
8. This does not preclude a large-scale development fund campaign that is part of a larger university capital campaign.
9. See, for example, D. Chaudron, "Roles and Recommendations for Friends Executive Boards," *HR Focus* 69, no. 9 (September 1992): 3. Although the information provided here is for self-directed work teams specifically, the elaboration I have made here is appropriate for friends Executive Boards.
10. B. Kaye, "Advisory Groups on the Seven Cs," *Training and Development* 46, no. 1 (January 1992): 54–60. Again this business-related model provides a goldmine of ideas and opportunities.
11. M.S. Leuci, "Getting Started: Forming a Steering Committee," http://outreach.missouri.edu/moexpress/guides/guide4-full.html. Again, this is a specific type of friends executive board but I have adapted it for these purposes.
12. Ibid, with adaptations for these purposes.

4 CATCHING THE WEB

The Web is neither panacea nor Pandora's box, though in inexperienced hands it will mimic the latter before resembling the former.[1] As touching its use as a Friends tool, however, it may be critical. For any twenty-first century library, a Web presence is a must. For any twenty-first century friends group, a Web presence is becoming increasingly mandatory. A moment's reflection will reveal why.

COMMUNICATION AND THE WEB

The key to any friends group's success is effective communication. Communication about upcoming events, successes, needs, problems, and recruitment are all required. In the pre-Web days—yes, these days were reality once (and no, dinosaurs did not roam the earth at the same time)—finding time to do all the necessary letters, newsletters, flyers, and the like proved a near impossible task. All too often *something* had to be left out, proving a decided drawback for the group. With the advent of the Web, however, all one needs to communicate to Friends members, or potential members, is the site's address. Getting this word out is far easier than one might assume: inscribing the Friends' Web site address on one's business cards, letterhead and of course, all the search engines, works quite nicely.

This does not mean that other forms of traditional communication—letters, newsletters, and the like—are obsolete. Having a newsletter that one mails out, publishes over the Web —or both—is still very important. And when one begins the arduous task of advertizing the group, it is nearly impossible to communicate too much or too often. Once the Web presence is there, registering it with a number of friendly search sites ensures that prospects are able to get to your site easily and quickly.

The site serves a number of obvious purposes. Apart from communicating to members, it establishes a rapport with the library and situates you in the larger context of the entity in which the library resides (for example, the community or the campus). Furthermore, it allows others to learn from you as you learn from them. Lastly, as you recruit

> The key to any friends group's success is effective communication.

41

gifts or seek foundation support, you have a ready-made informational boilerplate to which would-be donors may be directed. Since the Web is ubiquitous, it's hardly necessary for you to come armed with much when you go to see important potential donors. One can easily download to a laptop a PowerPoint presentation and showcase away. Even some personal digital assistants (PDAs) allow the downloading of much Web site information for instant presentation, though of course it would be difficult to see.

Finally, the creation of a Web page is no longer the technical task it was less than a decade ago. The first Web page I ever did required endless hours of looking up codes, putting them into place, and testing them out. It involved writing things like: <HEADER> <BOLD> Friends Groups <BOLD> [Center] and so on, all of which had to be typed out meticulously. One false letter, comma, spelling, or even a space would spell disaster on display. If you messed up, it was back to the drawing board to begin again. The advances made in Web page creation are so revolutionary that any fool can put one up (and with a billion-plus pages out on the Web, it would appear most have!).

Suffice it to say that there is no technical reason why you should not create a Web page. If you know how to type—even if with only two fingers—you can create a Web page.[2] But is this all you need to know? Almost. There are still a few other things you need to bear in mind. At the end of this chapter are a list of Web packages that can be used for a variety of reasons. These are merely suggestions and some of them will doubtless be obsolete by the time you read these pages. By the time this book reaches your hands, at least a hundred other, equally impressive packages will likely be on the market. Software packages of any type are not like points of interest on a map. They are more like the weather forecast: always changing. Consider, to mix the metaphor, that the list is not the *vade mecum* but your soup *du jour* at the time of this writing. Some of these are all-in-one packages, others only for special-effects use. Remember that there are many less expensive packages than the ones listed. Indeed there are many HTML and FTP clients that are simple and easy to use.[3] What's more, they are often bundled with other software you may already have. The list at the end is more or less the Corvairs of Web software, with one or two Lexus thrown in. If you want a Ford or a Chevy, or even a Mercedes, there is much out there from which to choose. For most Friends Web sites, "shareware," free Web design software, can be downloaded from the Web. For the rest there is, well, there is MasterCard. Now, a few simple rules about creating a Web page.

CONTENT

Above all, content is probably the most important part of the Web page.[4] Content should include obvious things, such as mailing address, e-mail addresses, information about the Friends, its executive board and information about how to join. You should have a way anyone can join *online* if possible, made available through your secure Web site. This is important because it allows potential members to join the moment they come across the page. If allowed to reflect, most would-be members might forget, or put it off indefinitely. And so, *descensus facile averno*; easy is the descent into hell. Better to have potential members join while they are thinking about it than to rely on having them fill out a form and mail it in later.

Your content should be informative, easy to read, lively, and entertaining. This is neither a documentary nor a scholarly treatise. It's a way for those of a kindred spirit to join your enterprise and help out. The best way to do this is to get them to join, and the best way to get them to join is to "hook" them with an eye-catching phrase or an unforgettable line. Unforgettable line? Such as?

Some years ago, an editor sought articles on marital infidelity and what to do about it. He received dozens that were going to handle it this way, and dozens more, that would handle it that way, all severely pedestrian. Another dozen boasted an historical approach, while several made the case for a more psychobabble treatment. Then came the following query letter:

"Darling! How I long to have you in my arms, holding me, caressing me, lying listlessly while listening to the waves crash upon the crabbed rocks outside our window." The letter continued in this vein for half a page before the author indicated that marital infidelity would be treated from the woman's point of view, as women told the story themselves. Out of hundreds of query letters, you do not need me to tell who got the assignment!

The same is true of content on a Friends' page. There is a fine line between fun and energetic, silly and stupid. It's easy to fall into the latter without realizing it. The important point is to seek an open, friendly style and exploit if for all its worth. Remember that this is your first chance to make the right impression, and it may be the only one. You want to leave 'surfers' not only remembering your site, but also wanting to come back.

KISS.[5] The old saw, keep it simple, stupid, applies to content above all. The more complex you make your Web site, the harder it will be to maintain. If operated by volunteers, then simplicity becomes a necessary virtue. If a member has an interest in Web design be sure he or she knows the simplicity rule still applies. Nothing stymies a Web site more

---

> Above all, content is probably the most important part of the Web page.... Your content should be informative, easy to read, lively, and entertaining.

Some general rules about Web page content:

- KISS: Keep it simple, stupid.
- A picture is worth a thousand words.
- Keep your Web address as short as possible.
- Try to remember not everyone's computer has turbo speed.
- Look for that eye-pleasing appeal.
- Follow the one-screen rule.
- Plan ahead.
- Exhibit consistency.

quickly than its creation by a guru and its later maintenance by a novice. While the guru may be bored by the simple creation, a later novice will be equally exasperated with its maintenance. Remember, too, that when the guru moves away (whether volunteer or library staff member) another must "fill in" and he or she *must* be able to handle it. The temptation to build a really super-jazzed-up site is strong for some. But in the end, both appeal only to the professionally minded. The novice or amateur is not only unimpressed but also often frustrated by layers he or she must wade through to get to whatever it is he or she is seeking to repair or refine.

A Picture, a Thousand Words. It is true that a picture is worth a thousand words, and in today's inflated library economy (see serials) one may be worth 100,000 words. Pictures need not be overly complex or elaborate. Many 3-D images (though part of the software listed below) may not be useful in Friends library designs. Sometimes a picture is all that's needed to draw and hold the eye. Horace says somewhere that we are often made prisoners by the eye than by the ear. Two thousand-plus years later, nothing we have invented or discovered has made his statement less true.

www.southcarolina.rock-hill.university.library.dacus/friends/fundraising/~l-proxy/index.html. This may be advice too late to use by the time it gets around to you, but here it is nonetheless: keep your Web address as short as possible. For example, the Winthrop Web address where I work is www.winthrop.edu/dacus. That's it. This has a number of wonderful features but the best is that it's easy to remember. If you know the name of my library and the university, you know the address. Even if your address is long, or longueur, you may be able to shorten it by placing your site on a different server or by working with your technology guru. It's worth a shot to try to shorten the address. The problem with long addresses is that they are rarely, if ever, remembered. While some may argue that it's unnecessary with all the search engine and metasearch engines, I beg to differ. There will come a time when someone will want to know the address and a computer isn't nearby nor will that person have a Friends card to give out. Besides, if you have one like the fictitious one above, all your Friends cards will have to say "continued on back side" or some such wording to get it all on the card.

Working…working…working…working…Computers are funny things. They do just what we tell them to do, hence the expression GIGO: garbage in, garbage out. It's important to remember this. Let's say you have an award-winning Web site ready to "go public." You've been applauded by every teckkie in the business. All who have passed judgement on your site have awarded you their highest compliments. Then you call it up on a Friends member's computer and you sit and wait for the next three to five minutes while it loads.

> **TIP:** Keep your Web address as short as possible.

There's no doubt about it. Web sites are fun and the more complex we make them the greater the feelings of accomplishment. But that, after all, isn't why you've built a Friends Web site. Try to remember that not everyone has turbo machine speed. They may not be as "in to" computers as you are. The whole issue of waiting is a generational gap. Those of us over forty don't mind if it takes Google 15 seconds or 1 nanosecond to retrieve 3 million hits. But everyone under forty *does* mind, and some of them can be quite vocal about it.

The rule of thumb is to add up all the graphics on the page plus the page size.[6] Experts argue that the ten-second rule *as an absolute maximum* is a good one to follow.[7] In other words, the shorter the time the better. Once you get beyond that you run the risk that visitors will become either discouraged or bored and click out.

Look for that eye-pleasing appeal. This may seem repetitious but by this I mean don't clutter your site with too much information. The under thirty crowd have an expression: TMI: too much information. Typically, this is a "sharing" of personal information that was neither solicited nor wanted. Web sites can do that, too. You want to tell your 'surfers' *everything* you can, and all on one page. Pretty soon, the site goes from 12 point to 11 to ten, to nine and it's so filled with data and columns and blocks that reading it requires an intervening page to tell readers to begin in the upper right hand corner of the screen and read clockwise until they come to X, and then begin reading counter clockwise. Or, there are many scroll buttons (see next item) and other instructions. Soon, 'surfers' will despair of finding what they want and go elsewhere. See KISS.

The One-Screen Rule. At Winthrop, we try to limit our first Web page—the first one surfers come to—to one screen. What we mean by this is that everything we want to say will appear on the screen that comes up, *without having to scroll down*. Friends groups' pages should strive for this kind of brevity. Too many users will simply not scroll down. I know it sounds silly but surveys and user studies indicate that if it doesn't appear on the screen that users come to first, chances are pretty high they will not scroll down or click to another screen unless that information is what they seek. There are ways to get around this, such as adding drop-down menus or scroll-over buttons. This rule forces us to say whatever we have to say in as few words as possible, usually with the aid of self-explanatory buttons. It's a good rule to have.

Plan Ahead.[8] Although it may sound like a cliche, it is nevertheless important to remember. You'll save yourself a half day's work, a week's frustration, and a month's anxiety if you'll just take a half day out and plan, with pen and paper, your Web page. Whenever anyone around Dacus Library wants to change the Web page, our Webmistress begins to hyperventilate. After a point, blood begins to boil and it is not always hers. The trouble with Web pages is that they are like topsy: they just

> **TIP:** You'll save yourself a half day's work, a week's frustration, and a month's anxiety if you'll just take a half day out and plan, with pen and paper, your Web page.

> **Innovative Web sites:**
>
> - Bowling Green State University (www.bgsu.edu/colleges/library)
> - Brown University (www.brown.edu/Facilities/University_Library/friends/index.html)
> - Bryn Mawr College Library (www.brynmawr.edu/library)
> - Cleveland Heights-University Heights Public Library (www.heightslibrary.org/friends.php)
> - Norfolk Public Library (http://users.rcn.com/npl/friends.htm)
> - North Carolina State University (www.lib.ncsu.edu/friends)
> - Otterbein College (www.otterbein.edu/resources/library/Friends/index.htm)
> - Princeton University (www.princeton.edu/~rbsc/friends)
> - Public Library of Palo Alto (www.cityofpaloalto.org//library/support/friends.html)
> - Saint Anselm College (www.anselm.edu/library/aboutFoL.html)
> - Spring Hill College Library (http://camellia.shc.edu/byrne/friends.htm)
> - University of Minnesota Libraries—Twin Cities (www.lib.umn.edu)
> - University of Pennsylvania (http://the-friends.library.upenn.edu/portal/support_frame.html)

grow. What begins as six bullet points ends, a week later, as five hundred sixty seven screens. If you take the time to plan first and then turn it over to your Web guru, you'll end up with an excellent Web page, organized by a master, and a delight to all users.[9]

Consistency. While it is true in most cases that "A foolish consistency is the hobgoblin of little minds," it is not true about Web pages. Besides, when Emerson wrote the line, he could not possibly have anticipated them. You might want to think about templates.[10] Templates will give your overall Web page a consistent look that will grab the eye without poking it out. If you begin with a template, it will also organize all the same elements on each page at the same location. Nothing is more frustrating for the user (just think of certain OPACs where the "Next Page" button changes with each screen) than to think a button will be at one place only to find, after he clicked it, in another place altogether. Templates will reduce this tendency and keep the premature clickers happy. "Cascading Style Sheets" is

the phrase most tekkies use to refer to this. It allows style information to be saved in the CSS file or in-line to achieve the sought-for consistency on all Web pages. (I am indebted to my associate dean Larry Mitlin for pointing this out).

OUTTAH SITES

You have purchased the software and you have gotten all your content. Your Web committee has met and now you are ready to go, right? Maybe. You could go ahead and begin reinventing the wheel, or you could take a look at other sites. Here are few chosen for their eye-appeal and clever design. All of these were viewed just before production. If my description does not coincide with them when you view them, that's only because they have changed. The great thing about a Web page (if you're not the Webmistress) is that it is a never-ending story. You will always want to make changes and add new features. Just be sure to keep in mind some simple advice given in this chapter, and you can change until you faint. Some of these sites are friends group sites, per se, and some are not. I have chosen them for their look and ease of use, not necessarily limiting myself to friends sites alone. For the sake of ease, I have listed them in alphabetical order.

BOWLING GREEN STATE UNIVERSITY
(www.bgsu.edu/colleges/library)

The "index" down the left side of the site allows users to click on whatever interests them without having to click their way blindly about the site. Both the "Activities" and the "Purchases" buttons provide more evidence of gaining friends and keeping the ones you have.

BROWN UNIVERSITY
(www.brown.edu/Facilities/University_Library/friends/index.html)

This friends page is a studied design in simplicity. What is not so simple is the scroll bar to the left of the site and the symbol-laden toolbar across the top. Within the friends site, however, nothing could be easier than clicking on "Membership Benefits and Information," or "Newsletter: *Among Friends*," or "Greeting Cards & Gifts." All of these provide crucial information or direct visitors to desired places. The "Greeting Cards & Gifts" provide yet another clue of what else you can do with a friends site. Not everyone will join but many will buy cards or even gifts, thus achieving the overall goal of raising funds indirectly.

BRYN MAWR COLLEGE LIBRARY
(www.brynmawr.edu/library)

The friends site here provides no-nonsense detail and is a good example of an easily designed Web site. Note that even on the friends page some carry-over buttons unrelated to the library still appear. These take you back to the college homepage or some other key page, like admissions. It is a good idea for the library to be "integrated" in every bit of university life.[11]

CLEVELAND HEIGHTS-UNIVERSITY HEIGHTS PUBLIC LIBRARY
(www.heightslibrary.org/friends.php)

Apart from a crisp, clean opening friends page, the public library has added an animation frame with content on the right side. This gives the page an active, lively look. While some computer users may find that this page loads slowly on their computers, or not at all, for those who have the power to run it, it is a very eye-catching addition.

NORFOLK PUBLIC LIBRARY
(http://users.rcn.com/npl/friends.htm)

This library has made ample and excellent use of color bars as the navigator tool. Large subject bars across the top and smaller ones down the right side make navigating the site easy and pleasant. The "About Friends" page begins "Who? What? Why? How?" Each pronoun directs the user to a separate page with explanations for those seeking that information. As always, each word stresses what the library's outreach is and what the friends do to help the library in its overall mission. The explanations are neither long, nor involved, but pithy enough to provide the right amount of information for inquiring minds.

NORTH CAROLINA STATE UNIVERSITY
(www.lib.ncsu.edu/friends)

If you do have strong support and a strong membership, you can do a great deal without over-much pizzazz. The opening page is straightforward and to the point. Everything you need is right there and is fulfills the one-screen rule. Furthermore, you get the name of that all-important person to contact. The reason for membership is concise and convincing without going overboard. The "Author-in-Residence" button is a good example of how you can turn a big thing into a crowd-pleaser.

OTTERBEIN COLLEGE
(www.otterbein.edu/resources/library/Friends/index.htm)

Otterbein uses the library's picture as the key ingredient on its opening page. Moreover, the "Pictures" button gives visitors an idea of what they are missing, while giving members something to look forward to each time they visit the site. The "Bylaws" button also points to another important aspect. (Bylaws are treated in the Friends Group Starter Kit, part A.) Some visitors will click there to see what the terms of service are and what is expected of them. This saves countless letters that would have to repeat the same information. I imagine that many are told to go to the friends home page for more information.

PRINCETON UNIVERSITY
(www.princeton.edu/~rbsc/friends)

Friends of the Princeton University Library opens its page with a mission statement. The statement not only discusses what the friends are but also where the friends have come from. The page also stresses what the friends do, from programs to book publishing ventures. The page also stresses that the friends newsletter, *The Princeton University Library Chronicle*, is written *for the general reader*. What this tells the casual visitor is that he or she will not be besieged with library-arcana, but with well-written, informative pieces.

PUBLIC LIBRARY OF PALO ALTO
(www.cityofpaloalto.org//library/support/friends.html)

The Friends of Palo Alto Library use buttons down the left side of the screen to direct users. These drop-down buttons are repeated on subsequent and preceding pages. When this page was visited in the fall of 2002, a picture of the friends book sale greeted visitors to the friends page. Also on the page are instructions about how to make book donations for the book sale, the chief fund-rasing event of this group.

SAINT ANSELM COLLEGE
(www.anselm.edu/library/aboutFoL.html)

The friends page for the Geisel Library is simplicity at its best. There is nothing fancy nor technically explosive. Yet the page works quite well for anyone wishing to gain knowledge about the friends group there. The *Friends Forum*, the friends newsletter, combines straightforward information with human interest angles. For example, the page viewed in the fall of 2002 explained how staff managed to *tunnel* their way through snow to work. It also showcases a particular staff member pertinent to the story. Such stories humanize the work of the library on a level that anyone can understand and appreciate.

SPRING HILL COLLEGE LIBRARY
(http://camellia.shc.edu/byrne/friends.htm)

You do not have to be a large college or have lots of funding to create a Web page. The Spring Hill College Friends have done some spectacular things to attract Friends, too. They have listed an event that occurred nearly seventy-five years ago as a draw for helping today. If you can read the opening page without wanting to help, you obviously have not a library's bone in you. It is always a good idea to build new traditions while drawing upon older ones. Although the Web stresses individuality and has made community building somewhat harder (you don't have to leave your house), it doesn't have to be that way.[12]

UNIVERSITY OF MINNESOTA LIBRARIES—TWIN CITIES
(www.lib.umn.edu)

The curved line on the front page is clean, clear, and easy to read. When you scroll over the buttons ("Books and More" and so forth), more information appears. While somewhat difficult to get just right, it has the advantage of displaying a wealth of information in a small space. Moreover, the drop-down boxes below add even more features. There is nothing pedestrian about this look. When you first arrive, you think you have hit upon some futuristic site, not a library Web page.

UNIVERSITY OF PENNSYLVANIA
(http://the-friends.library.upenn.edu/portal/support_frame.html)

The Friends of Penn use some of their pages to record tributes to friends supporters, or individuals who have worked at Penn and made a lasting contribution. Obviously such pages change from time to time or may not appear at all, but the point is well taken. Any time a friends group can make a contribution to the community (both the academic one and the community at large) the friends should showcase it. There can be no denying that this is an excellent use of the space. Surprises abound in friends Web sites. A most enterprising one here is the use of "e-friends," a project that collects friends for fund-raising goals while informing them about upcoming events.[13] E-Friends can "click and join" and remain an e-friend without paying a membership fee, at least not immediately. But the "database" created is later used for fund-raising purposes. The site also boasts a "Friends Forum" where friends can "lurk" or actively participate in discussion with professors, authors, and others.

CONCLUSION

The advent of the Web opens up to friends groups the ability to make their cases on a continuous and ongoing basis, one Web page at a time. Web pages should be designed to reinforce the three Rs: raise money, raise recognition, and reach out.[14] Librarians and friends group executive board committees should come together to figure ways to best utilize these in a given library setting.

Raising Money. It should be obvious by now that raising money takes time, patience, and a little luck. If you have access to professional staffing, or if you have a position dedicated to this task, so much the better. For the vast majority of friends groups, however, there will be

> Web pages should be designed to reinforce the three Rs: raise money, raise recognition, and reach out.

neither. Access to professional staffing will probably come in the form of, "We'll assign someone to your area and when they are free, they'll assist you." Do not take this personally. This is just a matter of economics. When you go schlepping for dollars, the library is rarely on anyone's top two list. Consequently, you need to put to work "someone" who will always be there, making your case, even when you're asleep. That's the Web page. When you think about it even for a few seconds, you realize how invaluable this tool is. To reach as many people as the Web reaches in a given day would cost you hundreds, perhaps even thousands, of mass mailing letters. And while it is not free by a long shot, it does fall under one of those budget headings that will be funded regardless, so you may as well use it. But how is that case made?

It is made by spelling out what you are about and why you are even a presence on the Web. It is made by telling your "story," your reason for asking for funds in the first place. It is made by explaining in a few sentences how John Q. Public can help. What is so very useful about the Web is that this can be done all in one screen: your case, how one can help, and where to send the dollars. It does not have the same appeal as a person-to-person visit, nor ever the same effectiveness. But it makes that case to hundreds of viewers daily, hundreds your groups would probably never think to make the case to unless you mailed a letter to every resident of your county.

It also does this with pages that allow online contributions, whether in dollars (such as secure credit card pages) or in kind (where to bring books for the upcoming book sale). Of course, whatever you do, or however you use the page, you will need to consult with the University Relations/Development office/governing board. Use of such tools can be surprisingly rewarding. We have seen how the pages can tell of upcoming friends events, and, in a post-event fashion, tell about how well an event succeeded (and they all succeed if you get even one person to attend).

Finally, we have seen how some groups used their friends pages for online stores. This can range from the "crafty" to the "classy." Perhaps you have a number of capable folks on staff on in the friends group who could produce certain items to post for sale. Once you have secured the necessary intellectual property rights, and have cleared the sale with the appropriate on-campus departments, you're ready to "open shop" and see what the market will bear. In short, there are scores of ways to utilize the Web for fund-raising purposes. There is no limit, beyond imagination, the ways the Web can be used. For example, at Dacus Library, we advertized our community and university postcards during the city's Sesquicentennial celebration. The cards made a nice memento or gift for any occasion. The response was overwhelming. We sold more than five hundred sets of these cards.

> There is no limit, beyond imagination, the ways the Web can be used.

The classy might be an author who recently came to speak and left behind some autographed copies. Maybe it is a faculty member who recently garnered some special award or grant, or an institutional award that makes everyone who works there look better. Whatever it is, the idea is to showcase the friends and the library.

Raising Recognition. We can understand this term in at least two ways: Recognition of your friends group, and recognition of individuals in that group. In the former case, what you are trying to do is showcase the group and what it does. This can be done either by spelling out what you do, or by downloading pictures to the Web. The latter is a bit more technically difficult, of course, but far more effective. For example, you might have a series of pictures that show a recent event. It might be pictures of the recent "Friends race" or an author who was recently on campus. It might be the arrival of new and important equipment or a special library and/or friends award.

Individual awards can be made online as well. We have seen how friends groups memorialize those who have passed on, or those who have provided numerous years of active and productive service for the friends or the college, university, public, or special library. An award can easily be created online that appropriately recognizes the individual while also showcasing the friends group.

Reaching Out. The friends page can also be used to reach out to potential friends, or have them reach back to you. The University of Pennsylvania example, cited above, is a case in point. Not only does it expand the Friends membership rolls, but it also provides much-needed spadework for future fund-raising. You can also reach out in other ways. Why not, for example, have the friends Web site address listed on the Dean or Director's business cards, as well as the library staff? Why not add the line on the official library stationary? Above all, be sure it is on every library publication so even if there is a non-acquisitive appeal, there is still a chance that one person in a hundred will want to see what that address is all about and surf by.

You can also reach out to your own constituents, and by this I mean faculty and staff. It is always surprising how often, and how frequently the library's "own neighborhood" is overlooked or forgotten altogether. Do not let that happen to you. Be sure you have canvassed them early and often. They have as much at stake in the success as you have, so be sure that they have been duly informed.

Growing and cultivating a library friends group is hard work. It requires patience and perseverance, and an unwillingness to take no for an answer. But for all its hard work and effort, the friends groups on the Web is one place where everything gets easier, or is at least made to appear so. If there is a "don't" about friends that should be stressed repeatedly, let it be, "Don't underutilize the Web."

SOME USEFUL WEB-CREATION SOFTWARE

- Adobe GoLive CS
- Balthaser:FX
- Dreamweaver 4.0
- Dreamweaver MX 2004
- eZediaMX 3.0
- Fireworks MX 2004
- Frontpage 2003
- Photovista Reality Studio
- Ransen Gliftic Version 3
- Sunburst Web Workshop 2.0
- SWiSH 2.0
- ULead MySite 2.0
- Web Workshop Pro

AT A GLANCE

- Friends groups should have a robust presence on the Web.
- Communication about your group is key to its success and the Web provides access to that key.
- Content is everything on the Web.
- KISS: keep it simple, stupid!
- The occasional picture, strategically placed, can make or break your site. Try to create a balance between a few words and a few pictures.
- Brevity is the soul of Web addresses.
- A graphic-intensive site will slow down the rate at which your page loads.
- Web sites should appeal to the eye as well as to the the mind.
- Try to keep your information to one screen so surfers will not have to scroll down to find more.

> - Plan out your Web presence on paper to make its actual creation easier.
> - Consistency between pages is a Web virtue because it "brands" your site as belonging to your group.
> - A few sites are mentioned for their adherence to one or more of these suggestions.
> - The three R's: of a friends group Web site are raising money, raising recognition, and reaching out.
> - A few software packages for Web creation of one kind or another are listed at the end of this chapter.

ENDNOTES

1. For more on what one wag called "the howling wastes of the Internet," see my "10 Reasons Why the Internet Is No Substitute for a Library," *American Libraries* 32, no. 4 (April 2001): 76–78. Incidentally, this article is an ALA-sized poster, available by e-mailing herringm@winthrop.edu.

2. And not only a Web page. The great American novelist, Sinclair Lewis, typed on an old Royal typewriter and used only two fingers.

3. HTML refers to hypertext mark-up language, the "language" used for creating Web pages. This refers to the codes that make the words appear on a Web site in various formats, fonts, and appearances. FTP stands for "file transfer protocol" and refers to the protocol the Internet uses to send files.

4. But don't take my word for it. See, B.E. Keiser, "Tips for Enhancing the Value of Your Web Site," *Online* 25, no. 6 (November-December 2001): 40–53.

5. Only after I wrote this chapter did I discover that Richard Murphy had already addressed this issue in, "Step-By-Step Guide to a Successful Web Page," *The School Librarian* 50, no. 2 (Summer 2002): 202.

6. P. Wilson, "Ten Ways to Improve Your Web Site: Things You Can Do Today!" *Public Libraries* 41, no. 3 (May-June 2002): 147. While this is about a library site, it can be easily adapted for friends groups' Web sites.

7. Ibid.

8. A very good discussion of these and other points can be gleaned via M. Seifert and P. Beaman, "McKee Library Web Site Development." ASDAL Presentation (June 21, 2001). A slide show is also available at www.asdal.org/minutes/mckeewqebsite.html.

9. See also W. Terry, E. Greenblatt, and C. Hasert, "Build It So They Will Come: Blueprints for Successful Webpage Development," in *Head in the Clouds, Feet on the Ground*, L.R. Rossignol, recorder. Available through the Haworth Document Delivery Service at getinfo@haworthpressinc.com., 529. See also, B. Keiser, ibid., 40–41. Finally, H. Jobe-Web, "Creating a Web Page," available at www.marshall-es.marshall.k12.tn.us/jobe/wepage.html. J.R. Veldof and S. Nackerud provide another excellent discussion in "Do You Have the Right Stuff? Seven Areas of Expertise for Successful Web Site Design in Libraries," *Internet Reference Services Quarterly* 6, no. 1 (2001): 13–35. This covers everything from planning, to content, to resources.

10. H. Jobe-Web, 1.

11. While this may seem like a stretch, consider the South Carolina predicament. Some years ago performance funding was added. It began with something like thirty-seven items, some of which were broken down into two, three or even four parts, meaning, of course, that there were really more like seventy or eighty measures. Colleges and universities were asked to meet these standards and were given a "meets" "exceeds" or "substantially exceeds" rating. Guess which academic unit received no measurement at all? That's right, the library. Because libraries were integral to the process they were not measured. Since this often proved to be "additional" funding that could amount to more than a million dollars, proving the library's worth was critical.

12. R.D. Putnam, *Bowling Alone: The Collapse of the American Community* (New York: Simon and Schuster, 2000). Putnam discusses how the Web has reduced the need for us to communicate with one another. Yet this page, when done right, ties visitors right back to the "necessary things" for strong community-building.

13. The project was showcased in "Using the Web to Find Old Friends and E-Friends," by A. Corson-Finnerty and L. Blanchard, *America Libraries* 29, no. 4 (April 1998): 90–92.

14. D. King, "Three Rs of Web-Based Fund-Raising," *New Library World* 102, no. 7 (July 25, 2001): 265–69. I have adapted the explanations without reference to King's article.

5 MARKETING YOUR LIBRARY

> Libraries usually hold a positive place with people. They are the bedrock of our cultural and intellectual civilization. .... Like mom and apple pie, librarians have long been considered unassailable icons of cultural and moral worth. The key is turning passive approval into active support.

Shouldn't this title read, "Marketing Your Friends Group?" After all, this is a book about *Friends Groups*, not libraries. Right? Wrong! Read on.

Libraries usually hold a positive place with people. They are the bedrock of our cultural and intellectual civilization. Every librarian and friends member knows this, and so does anyone else who has ever used them for any length of time. Without this abstract conservation by libraries, nothing would be left of our intellectual culture (or any other culture) but the immediate, the now.[1] Similarly, everything librarians do and libraries proffer (or very nearly everything) registers a high degree of satisfaction among our mostly adoring public. Like mom and apple pie, librarians have long been considered unassailable icons of cultural and moral worth. The key is turning passive approval into active support.

Growing up, almost no child in America, or anywhere else for that matter, has to be taught to cherish libraries, or even to cherish a few librarians along the way.[2] Children run to them from the first time they are bought to the doors, authors routinely sing our praises in the Prefaces to their books. Some municipalities (and universities) may even protect libraries even during economic downturns.

For most of this country's existence, the local library was almost as common as the local house of worship. The two were never, of course, mistaken for each other, but both were established as near-equal community icons. Middle America had two representative symbols of its everymanness: the church steeple framed by those proverbial autumn leaves, and the local library, that acted, more often than not, as the backdrop for the collective cultural consciousness.

Almost no one will disagree with these sentiments. So what has this to do with friends groups and what has this chapter to do with this book? Some will doubtless say "nothing at all," and if you're one of those, go on to the next chapter. But I include it here for two reasons. First, libraries are really what friends groups are all about. They are not so much about the group itself (although that is true, too), as they are about *what* the groups represent, what they stand for. Friends who do not like the library, or know very little about it, will not be friends for long. Members who know much about what they are touting will make the best ambassadors for the entity to which they attach their allegiance.

> **TIP:** Remember: Market the *library*, not the group.

The second reason has to do with what we in the library world do not do enough of, and that is marketing. Call it an eccentricity if you wish, but it remains true nonetheless that libraries and librarians do not market themselves as much as they should. They try to, usually after the fact: after there are severe budget cuts, furloughed workers, cancelled periodicals, or laid off workers. *Then* we become very aggressive about marketing, too little, too late. What our efforts do then is preserve what is left, not reclaim what has been lost. Suffice it to say that this chapter is a clarion call to begin now to save it all.

I have written this chapter from the point of view of the library. If you feel it should be written from the point of view of the friends group, then insert that phrase wherever you see the word library. But I have intentionally taken this perspective, based upon the premise (or the eccentricity if you like) that it is the *library* that needs marketing, not the group. Make the library preeminent and the group will follow. In the end, this chapter is for presidents of friends groups *and* for those who run libraries.

RESISTING OUR HISTORY

The above familiar history may help explain why librarians have long resisted any marketing of the library's inherent value. Oddly, when economic distress finally caught up with libraries, they often remained grumblingly silent while branches closed and staffs were reduced beyond even the "bare-bone essentials." For some librarians, marketing (along with fund-raising) was something *someone* else did about *another* business enterprise, but definitely not by them. The seventies, eighties, and nineties witnessed skyrocketing journal inflation; and the new millennium ushered in rising costs of all materials while adding yet another with which to contend: the delivery of electronic materials over the World Wide Web. It is hard to name a more service-oriented group than librarians. In fact, we may be unparalleled in that regard. Perhaps this explains why (though it is beginning to change) for all our well-deserved praise and adulation, we lamentably and routinely flunk Marketing 101.[3]

> Our response must be *proactive*, especially with regards to finances.... We need to market our services, our resources, and our successes.

The good news is that some librarians, and therefore their friends groups, are waking up to this dereliction of duty. After remaining *reactive* for three decades, some are slowly coming around to realize our response must be *proactive*, especially with regards to finances, or lack thereof. Amid talk about libraries becoming obsolete because of the Internet, budgets being cut, hundreds of subscriptions being cancelled and staff being laid off, we are ever so slowly becoming aware of the advantages that marketing provides for what we have and what we do. Public libraries more quickly and readily than their academic counterparts have understood this, probably owing to their greater sensitivity to market fluctuations, that our story needs to be told, often, everywhere and anywhere.

For example, we are slowly coming to the conclusion that even for our most ardent fans, the fact that we often pay upwards the cost of a new Kia for *one* journal is not common knowledge. Furthermore, we are beginning to understand the simple "fact" of being a library, public or otherwise, may not be enough, may not be "the whole story." Slowly, librarians and friends groups are coming to understand that we need to tell the rest of the story. (with apologizes to Paul Harvey). We need to market our services, our resources, and our successes. The effort needs to be a concerted one; hence, this chapter encourages *both* the library and the friends group to market the common commodity.

SERVICES

Just what are your library's services? This seems obvious but it often is not. Once you know this, a friends group may be the best way to help "publicize" it. Key to the services are people. Librarians are trained to help people find things. We help people find whatever it is they are looking for, wherever it may be. If you stop and think about it, some businesses offer the same sort of service but never free—at least "free" in the sense that there are no charges at the time of the service—the way it is in almost any library in the country. Imagine walking in to the local Home Depot and being able to take home with you an expert in home repairs. Of course you can, but there is an attendant cost. Yet, when you walk into a library, you can have your own personal research assistant to aid you *every* step of the way, free of charge, or you can take home with you the best available information, again, free of charge.

More and more libraries are providing 24/7 reference service through computer-assisted, "real time" help. What could be more useful than getting someone to walk you through the often arabesque world of online databases and Internet search engines while you sit in your pajamas? Many libraries offer just this service but how many know about it? We also consult for nothing an hour, provide information on rare book collecting, give expert genealogical advice and even, in some circumstances, assist patrons in finding the right medical and legal information to make an informed decision. Add to this resumé assistance, term paper counseling, finding that elusive lost footnote, the store that offers X, and a host of other services, and pretty soon you will

> Librarians are trained to help people find things. We help people find whatever it is they are looking for, wherever it may be. If you stop and think about it, some businesses offer the same sort of service but never free—at least "free" in the sense that there are no charges at the time of the service—the way it is in almost any library in the country.

have more than you need to market to just about anyone living in your community.

Every existing library offers some or all these services and more. Furthermore, if these services were *not available* through the local library (whether special, academic, public or a combination of all three), patrons would be shelling out tens of thousands of dollars for even one such service. What's more likely, however, is that most would not have it all. Add to this all of the friends events—book sales, interesting speakers, autograph sessions and more—and you have a warehouse of activity available to most residents free of charge. It is high time that we shout these things from the rooftops rather than quietly carry out our work with little or no fanfare.

Some libraries still offer free meeting space (though it is true that the politicization of this space in recent years has constrained some). Book clubs, civic and church groups, bluestocking clubs, and clubs that defy description come to our buildings by the dozens every week. Of course, we all know libraries offer these numerous services, and so do those groups who avail themselves of them, but does anyone else? Additionally, outside the home, libraries are responsible for a significant percentage of all Internet service.[4] Imagine what this means to those who cannot afford it, or who, for whatever the reason do not want to pay for it themselves. We provide search engines, printing services at mostly *below* market cost, and special assistance. Try to get all that at the local Kinko's for free. If these are not indispensable community services, I am not sure how they would be defined. Friends groups can help make these more widely known for what they are: indispensable.

RESOURCES

Let us begin with the book and journal collection. What librarian has not filled out an insurance form on even a small collection only to realize that its replacement would cost millions of dollars, and that conservatively estimated? Even in academic libraries, many best sellers are available, especially nonfiction best sellers, for their patrons.

Not only do we house the newest and the best resources, but we also offer the best of all ages. Of course, many homes have the *Complete Works of Shakespeare* and probably several translations of the Bible. But do they also have the complete works of Chaucer, Gower, Johnson, Voltaire, and *every* translation of the Bible, Greek and Hebrew texts, the Vulgate, and just about every commentary published? Again, we librarians know we have all this, but do our communities, our friends groups? Need the latest census report? How about the *Background Notes* on Iraq, or the latest *Country Study* on

> Not only do we house the newest and the best resources, but we also offer the best of all ages.

Afghanistan? It is all there at your local library. Try getting that *today* at your local travel agency. News reporters in every community turn to the library for statistical data complete with accurate explanations and navigation expertise. When you turn to your shelves at home, do you have the last twenty years of the *any* almanac? The last two?

Then there are our journals, everything from *Time* and *Newsweek* (including every one of its back issues*)*, along with newsletters, *People, US, The Journal of Sociology*, and thousands of others. These are conveniently arranged on open shelves, and there is nearly always someone there to help patrons find their way around. Nearly every library in this country can point to dozens of "regulars" who come in every week if not everyday for newspapers, both local and ones from around *the world*. Try adding up what this would cost if you were to try to replicate only one-tenth of this at home. Bear in mind this only begins to scratch the surface of the myriad details, information, and data available at even the smallest of libraries.

Databases are still, for the most part, a free resource, especially if patrons come to the library building. Buying even one database—say *Academic Universe* or *Infotrac*, assuming one could buy an individual subscription—would be out of reach for all but the wealthiest of patrons. Even they would find it hard to meet the monthly expenses of just two or three, much less *dozens*. We offer the latest in science, technology, political science, and medicine. Does your community understand this well enough to associate these services with *your* library?

SUCCESSES

Our successes are often more than can be named. Patrons come to libraries daily asking questions that could not be answered anywhere else, even if one were to spend hours online. If you haven't been keeping track of these successes, now may be a good time to start recording them. You'll be surprised just how many will add up in a week's time. Every library can point to a story such as this: a given patron who comes in every day to read the *Wall Street Journal*, or to check an overseas newspaper. Have you ever marketed this? Some may argue that many of these are available online for a nominal fee and this is true to a certain extent. But try getting last year's, or last month's, or even last week's issue at a nominal cost; and you'll see just the mountain of resources and services put at patrons fingertips without fanfare.

The purpose of this small survey is to show that libraries have a great deal about which to boast. It also shows just how much libraries have provided *for years* without ever saying a word about what they do, or how much they contribute, to each community member's welfare.

> Libraries have a great deal about which to boast.

COLORADO LIBRARY MARKETING COUNCIL

Thankfully, this story is beginning to be told. The Colorado Library Marketing Council (CLMC) is just one example.[5] The Council developed out of the state's Governor's Council on Library and Information Services in October of 1990. Out of this conference came a growing awareness that librarians and libraries needed to "market their services more aggressively."[6] The progress had been steady, methodical, and successful. Programs in 1992 and 1993 focused on marketing the message and getting that message across. By working with the state's five library associations, the CLMC has been able to equip Colorado's libraries and librarians with the tools they need to make their case directly to their public. One solid success of this program has been the growing realization that librarians would have to retool, not only to market better, but even to do their jobs more effectively in an ever-changing library marketplace. The CLMC's Web site (www.clmc.org, providing online courses beginning in 2000) provides a wealth of information about marketing libraries that can be readily and easily adapted by any friends organization in any community.

Colorado librarians have also learned that marketing is "risky business." What will doubtless come about when any friends group undergoes this process is the fact that "business as usual" must no longer remain "as usual." For example, canvassing customers at the local "7-11" may not be first on *any* friends group list of things to do. But as Colorado librarians discovered, it became a necessity to tell their story. Surveys and other instruments, some conventional and some not so conventional, have been used by librarians using CLMC to better reach their clientele.

What Colorado librarians have learned is what every friends group that eventually tries it learns about marketing: it's not a one-time venture. One has to be ready to repeat it year after year in order for the message to be effective (and the ineffective ones discarded) as well as honing to a fine art what one hopes to teach the community about library services. It is simple when considered thoughtfully: ditties we hum subconsciously, and phrases we recognize as second nature, are generally brought about through marketing. We may *think* we are not influenced by these things, until we open our closets or cabinets and see the success of those efforts first hand. The same *can be* true for libraries, though they will not end up in our cupboards. We see them everyday but not as our patrons do, even those who use us irregularly. It is time we make the case intelligently *and* frequently.

Perhaps one reason friends groups (and librarians) have been slow to utilize the research gleaned from marketing is its bad associations in our minds. We may recall that poorly done local commercial that later became a cult classic of kitsch. Or we may see in our mind's eye that guy in a plaid sports coat (and matching pants) trying to get us to buy this or that used car. But marketing is really much more than that, and it is up to friends groups to use whatever tools we have at our command to sustain and improve libraries for our clientele.

BEGIN WITH THE MISSION STATEMENT

The best way to initiate the process is to begin with the library's mission statement.[7] Once this is understood the friends group can then use the mission statement to identify target groups, develop ways to reach them, plan the process, and evaluate what one has done.[8] At Winthrop University, for example, we turned this process over to marketing students in our College of Business Administration. Students worked on a semester-long project and it culminated in about a dozen marketing plans, parts of several of which we have chosen to implement. What better way to determine your target group than to get the target group to tell you what appeals them. The plans we have chosen to retain all follow a familiar pattern, and one that is commonplace in marketing lingo: the four Ps: product, price, promotion, and place.[9] The product in libraries is obvious—our resources, services and people—but it may not be so obvious to others. How often have faculty called you with a "hot new journal" that you have been taking for years, or patrons complained that the library really must get database X when it is has offered it for more than a decade? Obviously we haven't made a strong enough impression on our clientele.

FRIENDS GROUPS "SELL" THE LIBRARY

Friends groups will need to do the same. They need to realize that the product they are "selling" is no different from what the library itself is trying to "sell." Think of the friends group as the library's private marketing agency. While "branding" has become commonplace in marketing, it should not remain alien to libraries. As Lee points out, it is already becoming part of the library with ALA's "READ" posters and its new @yourLibrary project. Friends groups may find branding difficult at first but if they will think about it long enough, a "brand" will emerge.

> Think of the friends group as the library's private marketing agency.

Twenty-five years ago the friends program at the first library I ever worked in had never heard of branding. But after two highly successful friends events back-to-back, we "found" our brand. Without really thinking about it, our friends group offered porcelain mugs at the first friends event and chose as the imprint the barely readable seal that towered above the library's front doors. It was so faint that we had to get old photographs to make sure it said what it appeared to say. A dove descended and beneath its descent was the Latin phrase, "*Lux lucet in tenebris*," light shines in darkness. The group used this on mugs for the first two events. It did not take long before many patrons who wanted the mugs as commemoratives for our annual event would call and ask about the "coffee cups with the dove" on them.

Place is less a problem today than it once was before the Internet, but place still matters and it is important that friends who market their group and, in turn, their libraries, understand this. Groups will want to be sure, now perhaps more than ever, that when someone encounters their group on the Web, they will know it is *their* group. Even with the Web, you want your patrons to recognize your library in their community.

MAXIMIZING YOUR WEB-BASE MARKETING

There are ways to maximize your *Web* marketing potential, and numerous helps stand ready to do this.[10] Some differences do occur and a few of these have been touched upon in Chapter 4. But groups who wish to sell products would do well to pay close attention to the spate of books available about using the Web to sell items.

MARKETING YOUR LIBRARY

> Librarians who not only take a leadership role but also see to it that their friends groups do the same will only be that much farther ahead of the game when it comes to fund-raising.

We have talked generally about marketing and mentioned a few principles, but now it is time to get down to brass tacks. For those of you who wish matters were not like this and find the whole topic of marketing and libraries repugnant, skip to the next chapter. Before you do, however, one reminder: wishing does not make it so. Librarians who not only take a leadership role but also see to it that their friends groups do the same will only be that much farther ahead of the game when it comes to fund-raising. Many librarians are finding the profession we entered twenty or more years ago *vastly* different from the one we find ourselves in today. Welcome to the world of change, and whether you know it or not, that world is yours if you are in a friends group. It began when computers waltzed into the library in the early seventies. Our tried and true professional prejudices about formats have now been dashed to bits, our easy rules about cataloging shaken (how do you catalog a Web site, and should you bother?), and our comfortable notions about annual budgets devoured by skyrocketing inflation and the multiplicity of media. We have one verity left to us and it is not an easy one: we can be certain that what we know about libraries today will change in a few years, if not in a few months. Like Heraclitus, from this day forward, librarians will know only flux.

So, for the rest of us, what are some principles of marketing libraries?

PRODUCT OWNERSHIP AND TOUGH SELLS

Libraries are a tough sell. This may seem like reverse psychology but it is not. Stop and think about it. Every library can produce a warm fuzzy, but no one really owns it. Like air, no one really owns it, or rather, *every* patron who walks in the door. While this might make one think product ownership is easy, it isn't. When everyone owns it, no one does. Think a minute about your demographics for a moment. A library's demographics might look like this:

- Age: 3-95
- Race: all
- Households: everyone of them
- Household Incomes: 0-millions
- Sex: evenly divided between men and women
- Geographic location: in town and around the world

The bad news is that it's hard to target *one* group. The good news is that it's hard to miss any target group you choose. So the first principle might be this: look for the good in what you do.[11] The trouble with marketing something everyone owns is that *everyone else* thinks the other person is supporting it. The trick is to think about what you do, encapsulate it in a few easy-to-remember points, and then begin the process of selling it to your clientele—*all of them*.

But if everyone owns it, isn't it already sold? Not really. It is not until those few or many actually put *their* money into *your* friends group. Most patrons already know why they come to the library. What they do not know is why you need their money and therein lies the rub.

> A key principle of marketing libraries: look for the good in what you do.

> Most patrons already know why they come to the library. What they do not know is why you need their money.... Much of library marketing is teaching others about the cost of your product and how underfunded it really is.

> **TIP:** Conduct user-satisfaction surveys before attempting to implement change.

Much of library marketing is teaching others about the cost of your product and how underfunded it really is.

THE LIBRARY AS VALUE

In the end, "[M]arketing is the process of identifying prospects [patrons] and determining best how to turn them into customers [friends]."[12] The task is formidable but it can be done if care is taken how one goes about it. One especially important aspect is value.[13] In order to *market* a product, one has to convey to target groups why such a product is valuable.

For example, how often in the past year have you conducted a user-satisfaction survey *and* used it to change what's being done? User-satisfaction surveys are common in libraries. What may not be as common is *changing what you do because of what your learn even if it means doing something non-librarian-like*. While it's considered a colossal blunder in the marketing world, how many libraries, after spending a tenth as much money, would have cancelled an entire offering if it crashed and burned like the "new" Coke? Yet, the Coke company turned that blunder into a boom. These surveys can also be very useful in helping us establish our own market segmentation.

Even though anecdotal evidence is limited to small audiences, it is nevertheless such ideas that help friends groups understand what the library does and how it helps its clientele in ways not readily apparent. Moreover, it also provides solid examples of real value. It is up to friends groups to ferret out such examples and present them to potential donors to complete the cycle of successful marketing, unless of course your group plans to recruit all new members every year.

MARKETING LIBRARY NEEDS

Marketing library needs to create successful fund-raising is another way to exploit the gamut of publicity. The Friends of Redwood Libraries did this in a remarkable manner.[14] When a budget shortfall threatened this system with severe cutbacks, or worse, the friends began looking at their options. The group sent a letter to their six hundred members explaining that if everyone who got the letter gave five dollars, this particular shortfall would be avoided. The friends allocated two thousand dollars for the campaign and ended up spending nineteen hundred. The result? Nearly forty-five thousand dollars was raised, averting the budget disaster.

What makes the Redwood experience noteworthy, in addition to its obvious success, is the number of successes and failures within the campaign. First, the friends group recognized it had to have a budget for this campaign—following the old adage that you must spend money to make money—and stuck to it. But it also had failures. While they were successful in raising funds overall, individual attempts (for example, donations from professional organizations) failed. This roller coaster life cycle is nearly every company's experience with marketing, and further underscores why it's important to keep track of what you do. Some things will succeed while others will not. It's good to know what does and *does not* succeed for the next venture. One key to successful marketing is a willingness to revisit the same issue often, just to be sure that what worked one year is working the next. Marketing is not a one-shot, one-time encounter. It must be constantly revised, re-implemented and updated.

Marketing your group's library services and needs must take a backseat to nothing. We all have clienteles we must satisfy. In order to do this we must get feedback on the programs we now provide. This means examining marketing survey data (though those of us may not want to call it that). Many libraries may find that they are dissatisfied with the results of the data, with their efforts to improve, or both. But that speaks less to effectiveness of the ideas, and more to our execution of them. Not only are resources ready at hand to help, but so also are many resources available through FOLUSA, ACRL, and many other library organizations. It may be necessary to provide library training after hiring a person effective in public relations *but without a library degree*.[15] We can easily teach the one while we may not know how to begin with the other.

If all of this seems overwhelming, it need not be. We already saw in Chapter 4 how the Web can be used to this advantage.[16] Most changes in what we do will mean fine-tuning what we are already doing. For example, up-to-the-minute status reports on Interlibrary loans. Many may do something like this already. All we need to add is a simple report that we generate for ourselves anyway and get them to our "clients" who need the information far more than do we. There is no doubt that much of this talk about marketing and "clients" will leave some cold. It will prove better in the long run, however, if we can get over this before we discover that our clients have gotten over us.

BEGINNING THE MARKETING CYCLE: SWOT ANALYSES

You may be wondering at this point how your group can begin marketing its library. The best place to being is to find out if the library has ever done a SWOT analysis. If not, *now* is the time to do one. You may realize that marketing is important, even essential to your friends groups. You may also realize that you have something to tell your community about: library programs and projects, friends programs, local and regional events. The one lacking puzzle piece is where to begin. Discovering the strengths, weaknesses, opportunities, and threats of the library will provide the friends group the fodder it needs to feed the marketing machine.

> Discovering the strengths, weaknesses, opportunities, and threats of the library will provide the friends group the fodder it needs to feed the marketing machine.

Most libraries do these analyses routinely, but if yours has not, you need not fear for there is no better time to begin than the present. A SWOT analysis is an investigation into the library's strengths, weaknesses, opportunities, and threats. What comes out of this analysis will provide excellent data for a baseline marketing audit.[17] It is important that the library examine the "environmental forces" in order to enhance "an agency's ability to be proactive by looking at the short term horizon and considering the impact of changing…conditions."[18] It is also an important position for the library in its current environment, in a sense taking a snapshot of where the library is and placing it where it wants to be in the near future. Given that the library's current environment today is very different from what it was only five years ago, it's a good bet that it will not be in the same place five years from now.

Furthermore, the SWOT analysis helps the library assess what it has been doing, how those things it is doing well can be strengthened, and how those things not being done well, can be done better. It is helpful to remember during this process that if the services are not serving your clientele—your patrons—or not serving them well enough, then either the services should be stopped, or changed so that they are more successful. As you go through the SWOT process it should become obvious again why the library's head must be intimately involved in the friends process and further underscore why, in Chapter 1, we said that the director or library's CEO must be the main interface with the friends.

Strengths. What does your library do well? What is it that your patrons *always* come to you for first? This may not be as obvious as it seems. If it is your computers alone, then do not delude yourself, because they can gain *that* access elsewhere. Figuring out why your strengths work well will come when you spend time brainstorming your many strengths together. You will be surprised what you discover *together* as you go through this exercise. Writing everyone's thoughts on butcher paper or a grease board is also helpful. Whoever records this—and it probably should be the library's head—should not make any value judgments. These will come later.

Once completed, and everyone has said all he or she wants to say, try grouping these strengths into categories: services, programs, and the like. Once you have done this, have someone write everything down and circulate it among staff. It is best to do this over a few days as other ideas will naturally occur after a few days of reflection. Once everyone has agreed on what has been recorded, you are ready to tackle step two. Group your strengths into categories so they will be easier to assign later on.

Weaknesses. At first, these will be harder to come by so persistence will be needed. Like the Lake Woebegone effect where all children are above average, it will be hard to pinpoint real weaknesses for it is the *other* libraries, not yours, that aren't up to snuff. The first to emerge will be easy ones that may or may not be actually true weaknesses: low budgets and low salaries. Even if you assume these are legitimate weaknesses (and they undoubtedly will be) more will come. This is why it is important to get feedback from other sources: patrons of every description and category. Without these important sources, your weakness may only be strawmen.

One very beneficial aspect of examining weaknesses is not only that they eventually come after a few false starts, but also that staff are quick to resolve them. If the library head were to say, "I want you to do such and so," the response might legitimately be, "How can I? I'm swamped as it is." But if these are singled out through the SWOT process, the likelihood that they will be undertaken and solved is very high.

Equally important in this process are certain ground rules, such as no person or department is singled out in an inflammatory way, only *services*. As soon as someone says, "Circulation really doesn't do it's job when" the game is lost. Circulation personnel must now defend themselves and will inevitably launch a retaliatory volley against the person or the department (or both) that launched the preemptive strike. Establish these rules early in the process and all should go well. Curzon argues that a key to effective brainstorming is the separation of staff from their ideas.[19]

Another benefit of the weaknesses process is the understanding that each library has a way to go, has unreached goals. All of us know this but we may not know it operatively—just metaphorically, which is to say, not at all. This is especially true of staffs that have been together for a number of years.[20] You may find it necessary to ask "pointed questions" about certain areas in order to challenge assumptions or rock preconceived notions.[21] Using a book such as *Who Moved My Cheese* may help staff come to grips with the change-thinking process needed to accomplish this and other important tasks. Once it can be admitted that you are not perfect, beneficial and necessary change is at least possible.

One final word. Do not go fishing where there is no water. It is possible that only a few items will result. Perhaps there are areas you see that need change. Suggest one or two and if they are shot down, do not press them. Revisit them later. Do not demand they be included if they are not generally accepted.

Opportunities. Lastly, but certainly not least, are the opportunities. What are areas suggested by this process that you should seize upon? Most of the time, these will reveal themselves as both weaknesses and threats that you can reassign as opportunities. While not really earth-shaking, we discovered that *communication* was one area in which we could do better; so we listed a number of opportunities we could turn to our advantage (and of course to an eventual strength).

Threats. Equally important to the overall success of your marketing scheme are the threats that can come out of this analysis. In my years of doing this I have found that some librarians are not as keen on these threats as they should be. For example, *every* library must come to see the Internet as a threat to its own existence. While professionally we *know* it cannot really compete with a full-service library, we also know many of our strongest supporters see it as doing our jobs as well or better. Obviously then, threats are both real and imagined ones that need to be cited.

Other kinds of threats will also become obvious. For example, Barnes & Noble is not really a threat to a library. But the *service* it provides, as well as the setting, are. If this were not true, libraries would not be adding cafes in their foyers, and designing their layouts in imitation. Other such threats will also emerge, and all need to be listed.

THROUGH? SWOT YET DONE

Are you finished? Not yet. Although this is not obvious on a SWOT analysis for it is not part of the mnemonic, it should be understood as an important part of the process. With your categories in place and assignments made, participants in the process need to know everything possible about the strengths, weaknesses, opportunities, and threats. You may know what your collection contains, but do you know what it *should* contain? What is the latest technology? What parts of it will you use or ignore? Why? A SWOT analysis will help you identify what you need to do to move your library into the future. This process may take several weeks and will yield not only more strengths once it is complete but should also reveal more weaknesses, opportunities, and threats.

For example, when we went through this process, we learned how more and more libraries not much larger than our own, were moving into 24/7 reference services. We wanted to learn more, and the group in charge of Reference Services did just that. They reported a number of aspects that while generally known, were not known well enough for us to make an assessment. After thorough research into this, we still did

> You may know what your collection contains, but do you know what it *should* contain? What is the latest technology? A SWOT analysis will help you identify what you need to do to move your library into the future.

not think it something we should divert scarce funds to. The exercise was not futile. This will occur with a number of items. Even if you decide not to use them, you should still list them as part of the analysis. Once this part is completed, and all that you wish to have incorporated is included, you are ready to make a final analysis. Research is critical to this success of this enterprise.

There is no such thing as overkill when it comes to marketing who and what you are to the people you serve. If this were true, you would never hear another bread, beer, or broomstick commercial.

NOW WHAT?

Some final points are in order. If the library has not gone through a "stakeholders" process, this may be the time to do that, as well.[22] One must judge carefully about information overload, but if staff have not thought through who it is they serve it will be impossible—or at least exceedingly difficult—to think through the process of marketing to target groups. Many of those to whom library marketing is aimed are, of course, stakeholders. Especially important is looking at each process through the patron's eyes. "One way to obtain information on how customers view the services they regularly receive is to put yourself in their shoes and approach the library from the point of first contact."[23]

Whatever you do, you will need a budget. It is just not possible to have a marketing plan without one. Within a university, this may seem easier than at first glance. Call your PR office and ask what you can do to help with this process. Show them your SWOT analysis and ask them in what ways you can aid the delivery of information about the university (and therefore your library) to the constituencies. It may be that you can coordinate deliveries of the information and pool your budgets. The important point is to try. Get out in the marketplace and market what you have.

TELL ME AGAIN WHAT THIS HAS TO DO WITH A FRIENDS GROUP

Now that you have all this information from the SWOT analysis what can the friends do with it? Only everything. This gives the group something to talk about, something to showcase, a drum to beat. Most groups spend a great deal of time talking about themselves and their programs and this is good. But there ought to be more; there has to be and this is where all this information comes in. While this analysis will make the library a better facility, it will be doing double duty by providing current data for the friends to utilize with foundations and granting institutions. It will make clear to the group who the stakeholders are and why. It will outline the boundaries for fund-raising and who should be targeted and why. In the hands of creative and energetic friends members, it will suggest limitless ways to plan new initiatives, complete old ones, and fund new enterprises.

CONCLUSIONS

It should go without saying that the main target of your marketing plan should be your chief funding source. For public libraries this will be the city government; for academic libraries, the university president; for special libraries, yet another funding agency. *Don't assume these entities are already with you.* This does not mean that they are against you, but one reason our budgets are low may be because we have not made the case very strongly with this natural audience. For example, if you are an academic library, what could be better than to have such a plan that has been endorsed by the Friends, themselves made up of alumni, faculty, staff, and students? If a public or special library, what could be more compelling than a statement endorsed by a friends group made up of citizens, influential community members, and others?

So, what are you waiting for? Get to work on your marketing plan today.

AT A GLANCE

- The centerpiece of any friends group must be the library it represents.
- Both friends groups and librarians have become too comfortable in their history.
- Financial constraints force libraries and friends groups to "think outside the box."
- One way to think outside the box is to see what marketing can do for both friends groups and libraries.
- What do libraries and friends groups market? Services, Resources and Successes.
- Some help is available to both friends and librarians via the model built by the Colorado Library Marketing Group.

> - Another outside-the-box approach is to glean initiatives for the friends group from the library's mission statement.
> - Friends groups may be uneasy with the idea, but what they are really trying to do is "sell" the library.
> - Groups can "sell" the library by adapting marketing techniques to the library and the group.
> - To market the library, however, one must know the "product," and to do that, one needs a SWOTs analysis.

ENDNOTES

1. There is a real sense in which the Internet threatens to undo the stature of libraries, what with its ten-year historical perspective and the erroneous belief that "everything" is on the Web. See www.winthrop.edu/dacus and click on "10 Reasons the Internet is not a library."

2. This may not always be true, however, as more and more librarians anger the public over the insane debate about Internet filtering. Filtering should be an easy call. If you think that you can explain why pornography should be protected, think again.

3. J.L. Crocker, "Marketing, Public Relations and the Academic Library," *New Jersey Libraries* (Summer 1994): 6–9.

4. "Part II. Internet Access and Usage" at www.ntia.doc.gov/ntiahome/fttn99/part2.html.

5. M. Cox, "Colorado Library Marketing Council: Giving Librarians the Tools to Market Their Skills," *Colorado Libraries* 27, no. 4 (Winter 2001): 37–40.

6. Ibid., 37.

7. D. Lee, "Marketing for Libraries: Theory and Practice," *Mississippi Libraries* (Winter 2000) at www.lib.usm.edu~mal/publications/ml/winter00/marketing.html.

8. Ibid.

9. Lee also refers to this commonplace parlance.

10. Four that come to mind are: C. Allen and B. Kania, *Internet World Guide to One-to-One Web Marketing* (New York: Wiley, 1999); J. Davis, *The Guide to Web Marketing: Successful Promotion on the Net* (London: Kogan Page, 2000); W.A. Hanson, *Principles of Internet Marketing* (Cincinnati: South-Western College Publishers, 2000); and A.C. Ekin, ed., *Marketing on the Internet* (St. Paul, MN: Coursewide Publishing, 1999). Obviously none of these are written about library Web marketing per se, but that is by design. Good marketing is good marketing regardless of the object.

11. See J. Spoelstra, *Ice to the Eskimos: How to Market A Product Nobody Wants* (New York: Harper Business, 1997). The point is not that this is a product no one wants but that everyone owns. Although the book is over-heavy on sports illustrations, it has a number of very good marketing ideas.

12. D.E. Gumpert, *How to Really Create a Successful Marketing Plan* (Boston: Inc. Publishing, 1996), 9.

13. R.K. Sass, "Marketing the Worth of Your Library," *Library Journal* 127, no. 11 (June 15, 2002): 37–38.

14. S. Hillman and J. Stein, "Hi $5 Campaign: A Fund-Raising Success Story." *Marketing Library Services* 12, no. 7 (October/November 1998): 1–4.

15. Ibid., 9.

16. J.L. Balas, "Using the Web to Market the Library," *Computers in Libraries* 18, no. 8 (September 1998): 46.

17. L. Cram, "The Marketing Audit: Baseline for Action," *Library Trends* 43, no. 3 (Winter 1995): 326–49.

18. J.L. Crompton and C.W. Lamb, Jr., *Marketing Government and Social Services* (New York: John Wiley & Sons, 1986), 49, quoted in Cram, 327.

19. S.C. Curzon, *Managing Change: A How-to-Do-It Manual for Planning, Implementing and Evaluating Change in Libraries* (New York: Neal-Schuman, 1989), 52. Quoted in Cram, 328.

20. This is neither the time nor the place to expand upon more than a brief comment. Tenure, at least in libraries, can be very deadly to the overall salubrity of this academic unit. Once people have been together for a number of years, they cease to see things the way they saw them early on. Moreover, like the former Soviet Union, they see no reason to change them, because there is no built-in incentive. See M.Y. Herring and M. Gorman, "Do Librarians with Tenure Get More Respect?" *American Libraries* 34, no. 6 (June/July 2003): 70–72.

21. S.N. Espy, *Handbook of Strategic Planning for Nonprofit Organizations* (New York: Praeger, 1986), 31. Quoted in Cram, p. 340.

22. I'm always astonished at what people can be offended about. In a recent meeting, one individual was bothered by the term "stakeholder" as it evinced a notion of capitalism. I make no apologies here. America, for better or for worse (I think infinitely for the better) is a democratic capitalist society, and by virtue of such, stakeholder is not only a well-advised term but one especially well understood in this context.

23. Cram, 332.

6 COMMUNICATING WITH YOUR MEMBERSHIP

When I first became involved with a friends group, now more than twenty years ago, communicating with the membership proved to be nearly a full-time job. Each month I tried to think of items, ideas, stories, and whatnot to share. And each month I would come to the same conclusion: how far would finances go to allow me to say what needed to be said, and how often? As then director of a small academic library any additional costs however small proved too large. But communicating with the membership was too important to ignore. Today, the issue is not frequency or even cost. All that remains today is the necessity of communicating.

Communication is a key ingredient—perhaps *the* essential one—to a successful friends program. Operationally, communication "occurs only when there are two associated information producing processes and the output from one process is the functional inverse of the other's process."[1] In shirt-sleeve English, as James Jackson Kilpatrick is wont to say, what I say (process) is what you hear (inverse process) if I say it well enough. The devil is in the details of that *if*. It is the difference between what is said and what is heard that creates ambiguity, for the two are often not the same. For friends groups, this process of communication is critical to the success of the group and, ultimately, the library to which it is attached.

KEYS TO COMMUNICATION

The point of which is that your communications with your constituency must be well-done, frequent, persuasive, and varied. This quaternion is neither exclusive nor exhaustive. Yet, it highlights what it is you should be thinking about when it comes to communicating with your friends membership.

Well-Done. Well-done applies to a number of things, not the least of which is the content. This has been treated before and needs not be belabored here. Well-done also has to do with the writing. Of course all aspiring authors are going to write the great American novel…tomorrow. Until then, however, we must have our newsletters filled with the

> **Keys to Communication:**
>
> - Find a good editor
> - Strive for professional productions
> - Connect frequently
> - Be Persuasive
> - Offer Variety
> - Provide Web sites
> - Send E-mail
> - Try Blogs
> - Consider E-zines
> - Remember Newsletters

kind of taut, snappy writing that intrigues while it interests. This is not the same thing as editing. This has more to do with style, with panache, with voice that allows something of the writer to emerge from the verbiage. Without this touch, this little added flair, your communications will likely be lost in a sea of other things that get tossed in the "junk mail" stack—a place that is often worse than the waste can, because it can still be read but of course will not be, and then gets tossed into the dustbin. It is like Tantalus, always getting near the grapes or the water, but never quite touching either.

There is bound to be within your membership at least *one* person who will be able to work with you to help you achieve this. If not, there is always the local college for a quick refresher course. This point cannot be over stressed. When sending out communications, nothing will make them less effective than for the writing to be full of solecisms, poor grammar, or awkward constructions.

Unless your group has money to burn, the chances are you will not be able to afford a professional editor—one who will correct grammatical mistakes while tightening style. More likely, you'll have someone either on staff or from your membership who can serve as the proofreader. Proofreaders are essential, but they generally look for glaring mistakes, not stylistic problems. Look for someone among your membership to undertake this assignment. Be sure that the person chosen can actually *do* the task. I have found that retired English teachers are excellent for this task. Self-designated editors/proofreaders may or may not be what you need or want.

> All of us need a good editor...Without such a person, you may overstay your welcome from the first word.

Find a good editor. All of us need a good editor. Tom Wolfe of *Look Homeward, Angel* fame would likely have never seen the light of day in print without his editor extraordinaire, Max Perkins. Perkins routinely took Wolfe's *million-word* ramblings and turned them into some of the world's great literature. This is not to discount Wolfe's genius, of course, but merely to underscore the necessity of having someone who will look at your words with unaffected sangfroid; that is, will cut them with a cold-blooded eye. Without such a person, you may overstay your welcome from the first word.

Well-done also has to do with the format, with the presentation. *Nothing is more inimical to friends communications than shoddy productions*. All too often friends groups will insist that the newsletter be produced for under one hundred dollars, and this includes printing. You must insist on putting your best foot forward. I do not mean erring in the other direction of slick glossy productions that bankrupt the funds before they ever come in. I do mean striking a happy medium between this and the two-sided mimeograph. Given the desktop publishing capabilities installed on most computers, newsletters can be done very well with a little time and effort. Remember the little things, like white space and eye-appeal, just as with your Web page.

Good communication with members must be richly varied. If every issue is filled with a plea for more money, chances are your membership will grow weary. Much to be preferred is the varied content that allows you to focus on services one issue, recent purchases the next. We publish a newsletter unrelated to our friends group called *Dacus Focus*, after our namesake, Ida Jane Dacus. For one year, we reported on the "Future of Library Services." This gave us a "lead" story every issue, and allowed our larger mailing list to include not only the friends, but also many others who could help us if they joined the friends. Out of that particular exercise, came a different kind of article that appeared in *Library Journal*.[2] By focusing on what we were doing as a library gave us the opportunity to showcase who we are as a staff. Something like this can provide your friends with fodder for its issues.

Frequency. Establishing frequency is like that commercial done many years ago on the rather private topic of regularity. In touting one product over traditional means, the announcer intoned, "With prunes you never know. Are three enough? Are six too many?"

As much as one can, try to schedule your communiqués in such a way that yours is likely to be one of few going to your membership. This is not as hard as it may seem. Some simple checking can make sure your friends newsletter will not get lost in the mountain of mail. This is easier for academic and special friends groups, harder with public library groups. In a public library, you can check with the city for communications that go out under its aegis. Avoid sending out something on or before the first or last week of any month when it is bound to get tied up with bills and junk mail. In an academic setting, work with your University Advancement folks to determine the best time to send out your communication so that it falls between regular pleas for help and general university news. The last thing you want is to have your special communication to arrive when many other pieces of mail will arrive on or about the same week, or when other regular features of community or institutional communications are standard deliveries.

Your membership should hear *something* from your group at least every other month (every month is even better). If you have an annual or semiannual event, then your "copy" for those times is already set. If the library is putting out something and the friends group another, then you really *must* coordinate these so that the one hand washes, not arm wrestles, the other.

Do not forget that when thinking of frequency one should not think of major outreaches alone. While more will be said on this theme below, you will want to continue to work the friends-building part of what you do by making phone calls, scheduling lunch (or luncheons) dates, and by sending letters and/or cards.

Persuasive. Writing persuasively takes not only time but also talent. Persuasive communication is "any message that is intended to shape, reinforce, or change the responses of another or others."[3] The technicality is important. Miller argues that there is, in a response, a changing, a shaping and a reinforcement.

At first blush this might seem impossible but it is not. Think again of commercials. Nearly every commercial seen on television does this subliminally. We are persuaded by them, for all their bluster and kitsch that we should buy brand X over brand Y. The same is true of friends communications. Of course many of your communications will be on the order of information—this is what we did and when we did it. But many others will be—or *should* be—on recruiting members or potential members, and all should strive, in advertisement-like fashion, to persuade. It is critically important to remember this when writing for your membership. Numerous community people stop me regularly to tell me that they always put aside our mail until later, when they can take the time to read *every word*. There can be no better or more gratifying praise. Will it generate funds? Perhaps. The first and most important obstacle, however, has been accomplished: getting heard.

Variety. Last in this series is variety. If you are to be successful, you must be ready to attempt to communicate in a number of very different ways. Do not have *one* approach alone.

This can be done by distinguishing between message and approach. Your message will be unified and nearly always the same. Your approach to that message will differ. For example, Gap uses a number of commercials about your people having a good time, dancing in khakis, hanging out in jeans or "chillin'" to some music. The "point" of these commercials may not be very evident but the concept is always the same: no matter what you're doing, Gap clothes make it more comfortable, better, chic, or whatever. The same is true for friends groups selling their libraries. There are a number of ways to convey the same message. The point is to use all of them.

> **TIP:** There are a number of ways to convey the same message—use all of them.

CHANNELS OF COMMUNICATION

While by no means meant to be exhaustive, here are a few means you should consider employing as communication outreaches: Web sites, e-mails, listserv, blogs, e-zines, newsletters, luncheons/dinners, and special mailings. A few words about each should suffice to underscore the importance of all.

Web sites. We need not tarry long here. In Chapter 4 I went into depth establishing the importance of the Web site. All that remains is to reemphasize that a) you must have one and b) you must make effective use of it. Next, join FOLUSA and you are immediately linked to scores of others who are doing the same thing your group is attempting to do. It also allows you to trade information, seek advice of others and "partner" with literally thousands of other friends groups and members around the globe. This connection prevents you from reinventing the wheel each year (or even each month). You are able to piggyback on the ideas of others, plagiarize madly (with attribution of course) the work of many, and brainstorm with hundreds who are seeking many of the same ideas. Remember, Web sites allow for that "best-foot-forward" approach. Since the Web site may well be most members' first association with your group, it allows them to know what sort of organization with which they are getting involved. They can find out how often you meet, what kinds of programs you have (and what went on at those events if you provide photographs), who is on your board, what your needs are, what your mission statement is and how your bylaws govern your friends groups. What might have taken a dozen pages to do in the "old days" is now only a "click" away while your group reaps the not inconsequential benefits.

E-mail. At first blush you may not think that e-mail is very helpful. But regardless of the size of your group, you can communicate with them through e-mail, especially if you establish a listserv. Even only five years ago, maintaining a listserv would have been too formidable and time-consuming a task for most librarians even to consider. Electronic mailing lists today, however, "accomplish faster, more easily, among more people and certainly less expensively than was previously the case."[4] Server software now exists that handles nearly all the management activities that once required a person with technical know-how. While the services are still not completely maintenance free, they may as well be. All the subscriptions, broadcast postings and the like are now managed for subscribers by sophisticated software that keeps track of everything. On most college campuses, a call to your IT person will generally yield a listserv, or something like it, in a matter of hours.

Listserv. A listserv allows friends to communicate with one another or with all the members at once. Think of it as having a board meeting at which every member in attendance may hold the floor for as long as he or she would like, interrupted only by the occasional comment from others. If you limit the listserv only to members in good standing, then you add yet another dimension to your membership privileges. We have all been witness to the value of listservs in other contexts. Imagine having this power at your friends disposal.

Listserv can be moderated, unmoderated, or broadcast.[5] In a moderated list, the moderator (obviously) reads all the messages posted to the list and then sends appropriate ones while rejecting others. While this may seem unwanted and censorious, it has the distinct and very positive advantage of making certain your listserv is not spammed, or is not dominated by individuals who have a rant-complex.[6] A moderated listserv will assure all users that only pertinent messages will go out, and only those that do will be on topic. While it may stifle discussion at first—who is she to reject my posting?—it will eliminate the very embarrassing situation in which you have to ask a given individual to shut up and stick to topic.

An unmoderated listserv, on the other hand, is, obviously, just the opposite. This of course takes almost no time on your part but your members are not only subjected to useful discussion, they are also subjected to the latest conspiracy theory and those tiny, hidden cameras that allow you to snoop anywhere in your house. And if you act now—well, you get the picture. One significant problem with unmoderated listserv is that often members will get online to one thousand two hundred messages from a membership of only three hundred. Once they have waded through seventy-five percent of them that are completely off topic, most will unsubscribe from the list.

Finally, *broadcast* listserv allows only one-way communications: from you to all the members, but not the members to you, or to one another. In many ways, it is the equivalent of an e-mail newsletter.[7]

After determining what kind of listserv you will have, your next decision must be who will host it. Again, on academic campuses, this will be your IT or library server. Public or special library friends groups will use their own servers. For example, Yahoo! Groups (www.yahoogroups.com) are useful for unmoderated groups. But be forewarned. Your members *will* be spammed by advertisements and those incredibly annoying pop-ups. And while when it happens (and it will) it will not be anyone's fault, your members may well get graphically-objectionable pops-ups as well. Since this is, for now anyway, the spider's poisoned bite that comes when anyone logs on because Yahoo! allows for objectionable distributions, your members will be one step closer to seeing what they may not ever wish to have seen. The other part of that question is whether your friends group can be distanced from such occurrences well enough for members to know this was *not* the Friends doing.

Yahoo! groups also allow for moderation via e-mail to the moderator.[8] Other hosts do not do this, but require the moderator to check the messages, which may or may not be something that the moderator will have time to do, or remember to check. Once you have chosen a host, then you register it and choose an address to which members can post. Suppose your library friends group is named Libertas. Your e-mail could be libertas@yahoogroups.com. At this point you will have to decide whether you will allow anyone to join, in which case you will leave it in the directories. On the other hand, if you require application and want to keep it private, you will want to remove it from the directories.[9] The setup for Yahoo! groups, or any of the other similar groups is very quickly managed. Members can join by subscribing to the list. This is generally done by adding to your broadcast e-mails instructions on how one can subscribe and unsubscribe.

Blogs.[10] One relatively new and potentially exciting way to communicate with members might be a friends-blog. Blogs are Web sites where one individual places on the Web issues to which any other individual can come to respond, both on and off topic. They are generally run by one person who sets up his or her blog with information to which others can respond. In the early going, these were (and many remain) political in nature. Why not a friends-blog for all the friends groups in your city, county state or region? It might be the best way for you and your members to share information on a given topic—in this case the friends—and vent any idea you may have on same.

E-zines. There is no rule that says if you do a print newsletter you cannot also have an electronic one. You can for example publish a newsletter and simply post it on your friends Web site. This is not an e-zine *per se* but it will serve the same purpose. A true e-zine is of course a newsletter than is available only online. *Slate*, for example, is an e-zine in its truest form because it can only be found at its Web site. The downside is of course those who do not have a computer, or do not have access to one, cannot see it.

Is this a legitimate downside? Yes, albeit a minor one. There will be many in your friends group who are over fifty and who have no desire to attempt the computer expertise needed to gain access to your newsletter. If communication is connecting with members, and half your membership will be left out by choosing this form, then it may be best simply to post it later, after the paper issue appears. As time goes on, this will, of course, become less and less an issue. The upside to an e-zine is the cost, or lack thereof. Suppose you have a membership of two hundred. Although small, you still have the not inconsiderable cost of mailing out that many newsletters. Moreover, someone must do labels for all two hundred, along with the task of sorting all those newsletters for the post office.

With desktop publishing, e-zines also allow you to present a formidable production, complete with color and at no real cost the way a color printed newsletter can be. Printing a newsletter with only one color is not cheap, even with the desktop capabilities now available. Delivering your newsletter electronically allows your full creativity even fuller expression. There is no reason even the smallest of friends groups could not produce a sharp, eye-appealing letter that will encourage current members and recruit new ones. Color is not the only issue either. Graphs and pictures are also very easily distributed by an e-zine. Of course you still need to bear in mind the loading times of your membership, but it is not *that* critical to know. A four-page e-zine with pictures, graphs, footnotes, and more—in short all those things you guard against in a print-based newsletter because of cost—are yours for the insertion.

The other advantage the e-zine has is its ease of production and correction. Miss a comma? Simply add it before uploading it, or correct it and upload again. Need to change a date after distribution? Simple, just resend. Get a donor's name wrong? Don't sweat it. Correct it with an extended apology. All of this can be done in a half-hour or less and the membership will be greeted the next time they log on with a new communication. "While a print format newsletter has a limited distribution," according to Boykin and Kross, "the Web version is accessible to anyone and everyone."[11] The only proviso I would add to this statement is that it is true to everyone who has access to the Web. While many do, not everyone does.

This brings us to a final key feature of e-zines: frequency. With an e-zine, all you have to have is the time to write the communication. You could send them weekly if you want to, though it is unlikely you'll have *that* much to report. Still, the ease of creation allows the issue of frequency not to be settled by dollars or time, but by news and willingness.

Although not a critical issue, friends groups should also bear electronic delivery in mind when thinking about longer publishing ventures.[12] Digitization and/or electronic delivery allows friends groups to undertake longer publishing ventures that they would never consider otherwise. Of course such projects have their own inherent difficulties and critics but it at least could be looked at for long-term follow-through.

Newsletters. Some call it old-fashioned but most people still respond to the conventional newsletter. Of course part of this is nothing other than praising an old thing because it is old. But there is another reason and it has been hinted at already. When any of us surf online and find something we want, we will read it online *provided it is no more than two pages*. Since we know this to be the case, why not send your membership something they will not have to "fish" for and will already be printed for them to view another time? Moreover, since many memberships, even today, will consist of persons age forty or over, a printed newsletter may still be the best and most effective form of communication.

If a friends member can be paired with a staff member, so much the better. There is nothing at all wrong with having coeditors, one from the nonlibrary friends membership and one from the library's staff. Having two editors allows rotation during the year, assures that there will equal or near equal shouldering of the responsibilities and can, of course, groom one or the other coeditors to take the primary responsibility for the next year, creating an instant continuity from one year to the next.

> Some call it old-fashioned but most people still respond to the conventional newsletter.

The idea of rotation also keeps the storehouse of ideas fresh and the perspective polished.[13]

You can follow the same style sheet in both the printed and the electronic newsletter, whether it is the *Chicago Manual of Style* or Kate Turabian's classic, *A Manual for Writers of Term Papers, Theses, and Dissertations*. What matters more is that both newsletters read well, or well enough to keep you from the ever-present niggler who will drone on about ending sentences with prepositions. Having said that, the newsletter must be alive with color and *personality*. Nothing will stymie your message more quickly than for your newsletter to appear to your readers as vanilla. You *must* find your voice, as the creative writing classes say, and find it fast. Once in place, you will hold your readership for as long as is necessary. That duration should not be more than a few years unless your writers are very good. Rotating the editorship allows that voice to change and remain vibrant.

Frequency and regularity are important to the conventional newsletter.[14] Since this newsletter is going to both those members who have an intimate connection with your library (such as staff or faculty), and those members who may set foot in your library once or twice a year, it is important that you *stay connected*. Frequency should be determined by your bylaws. You want your readers to *expect* to hear something from you and on a certain time of the publication: beginning middle or end of the month. Also, be sure that whatever it is you are reporting, you run it by your office of advancement or official fundraising arm. For example, you may be chomping at the bit to tell your members of a gift you have just learned about. But it may be that the announcement must be delayed, or never mentioned at all. By alerting everyone you will save yourself from embarrassment, and possible loss of the gift. Enough about content has been said earlier so that it need not be rehashed now.

For some newsletters, publication information is important.[15] This includes things like frequency of publication, editor, address, phone numbers and the like. If groups want to do something like this, there is no reason to prohibit it. But to require it is to ask more than is necessary. Of course it can be boilerplate information that can be "tagged" to every issued. But for most friends letters, the difficulty of getting one out far exceeds the need to have this kind of information. If someone wants to ask a question (or complain) he or she will find a way to make that known. Having to keep up with these changes for every issue is, for most groups anyway, much ado about nothing. What is more important is the presence of your snail mail (and Web) address.

THINK BIG

When you send out the letter, think big. Of course you will want to cover all your membership. But do not stop there. Make sure the Board of Trustees (whether the group is connected to an academic, public or special library) is on your list. If there are libraries in your area (regardless of kind) be sure they are on the list. Are there important figures in your community who should know about your group, such as the mayor and others like her? Then be sure those names are part of your mailing list. Are their big supporters of other cultural events in the community similar to your own? Include them on your list whether or not they are members. Are there political figures whose understanding of your situation is important? Make sure they get a copy. Also, anyone who has ever spoken at your friends group for any reason should be included on the mailing list. Finally, be sure you print a few extra copies, perhaps as many as fifty extra ones, for distribution to interested parties with whom you come in contact between newsletters. These make great information pieces for people your friends group may want to court over, that library staff see professionally or encounter at meetings. They are the perfect introductions to the group.

> **TIP:** When thinking about communication, THINK BIG.

The important point is to make your appeals in these communications, whichever form they may take, as evangelical as possible.[16] That is, everyone with whom you communicate are instantly aware of the passion you have for your group. As Arant and Clark put it, "It's meaning for academic [or any] library public relations has multiple implications for fund-raising, public service and promoting the library. It relies on aggressive outreach efforts that take librarians [and friends groups] out of the confines of the building and into territory of those that are trying to serve."[17]

For too long we (all of us connected with library service) have been building-bound. With the vast number of competitors we now have—Barnes & Noble, Amazon.com, Questia, and of course the World Wide Web, to name but a few—we can no longer afford to believe we are the only ones providing access to information. We must now become far more proactive about our situation, or be replaced. No, this is not a doomsayer's warning. It is highly unlikely that we will be replaced by the Web. Too much information on that medium is fraught with error.[18] But if we idly sit by and say nothing, a lie will eventually get to be the truth, or at least its simulacrum heard often enough to make its refutation nearly impossible. Although Arant and Clark talk about service in a particular setting—the academic library—they have much to say that is very much worth taking to heart: service to constituents, whether those be students, faculty and staff or members of a special clientele, or the general public at large.

In my own setting, an academic library, I cannot tell you the number of times we have received *urgent* requests for books, databases, or journals that we have *subscribed to for years*. Whatever it is we are doing, we are not doing it well enough to get across even to our dedicated users what we have, and what it is we provide. Becoming "evangelical," even proselytizing is the right advice.

Even advertising your group in special e-mails or routine ones has advantages.[19] Why not add a line or two in every communication about what you do? A "Did You Know?" segment at a routine e-mail will provide *some* advantages. Someone will see it and come back later to you asking about it. No service is too small or too insignificant *not* to showcase. But bear in mind that when you do your own surfing how much you hate to see annoying ads. Keep them short and to the point. Since you are advertising a service and not a product also keep in mind what you can and cannot accomplish.

E-mail ads on specialty areas can net huge profits.[20] While libraries are unlikely to be able to boast several thousand hits an ad, several hundred does not seem impossible. Of course those libraries attached to an institution may not find this possible if it jeopardizes their charitable status. All of this should indicate that the lack of plan is not the way to go.

Essential Rules for Effective Communication:

- be certain that you know whereof you speak
- remain upbeat and always take the high road
- be forceful while also being polite
- bear in mind your vulnerabilities
- tell the pros and the cons of any project
- consider risk carefully but do not let it stop you
- make your plans comprehensible to your clientele
- remember partnerships in communicating your group value

ESSENTIAL EFFECTIVENESS

When you go about your communications, a few important matters are essential for effectiveness. If you follow these rules, you can be certain that the message will get across. While the medium is not always the message, it does a lot to carry the meaning to your constituents. Keep this in mind as you contemplate these few simple rules. First, be certain that you know whereof you speak.[21] It is one thing to be excited and enthusiastic about your library's service; it's quite another to oversell the service or the friends group's ability to deliver. If you think the temptation would never be there, think again. Once your group is involved in a bond issue, a building campaign, or just trying to raise significant extra funds, the temptation to get to the results almost without thought to the means required can be overwhelming.

Second, remain upbeat and always take the high road. It is easy when talking about communicating about libraries to focus on what's wrong; namely, low, or even pitiful funding. Remaining upbeat can be a challenge that will depress even the most positive of Pollyannas. The combination of friends group members and library staff should be enough of a cushion between you and the dark night of despair.

Third, be forceful while also being polite. It is no good to argue the friends group's case if you are going to soft-pedal it. You cannot afford to do this and your program cannot afford to have someone who does this. Libraries have been traditionally weak-kneed about selling their services. The time has come to "get over" this and begin to act forcibly on the library's behalf. We need to lay to rest the stereotype of the milquetoast librarian forever.

Fourth, while remaining upbeat and forceful, bear in mind your vulnerabilities. If you do not address, for example, the threat the Internet poses to your services, you will not only miss an opportunity, but also leave you and your group open to failure. You have to address this in the best way you can. This goes for all the other threats you identified during your SWOT analyses. Some may wish to retort offhandedly that in doing so you will suggest weaknesses to your clientele that they have not even considered. It is better to assume your clientele is smarter than they are, as opposed to the opposite assumption.

Fifth, be sure to tell the pros and the cons of any project. If your friends group is going out on a limb, say so. If there are other inherent risks involved with what you are doing or are about to do, tell your clientele the truth. You need to be sure that your group not only knows what you are doing, but also why you are doing it. While not everyone will agree with every project, you set the tone for the group by taking advantage of this whenever you can. Of course there will be times when either the nature of the project, or the donors, or both, forbid any early announcement. But if you set the standard high, you will not have a hard time getting your support on board.

Sixth, do not let risk stop you, but consider it carefully. It is hard to make huge gains without some element of risk. That is the nature of just about any human endeavor. If you always fear risk, or assess it without measure, you will inevitably run into greater difficulties while courting certain failure. Twenty years ago, I worked with a friends program at a very small institution where *every* speaker's event was a risk, because we did not have the necessary funding in place to assure a successful outcome. One speaker in particular—an internationally known author and commentator—charged what was at the time an enormous fee. Although he cut the fee in half, it was *still* enormous to us, and would have been to an institution twice, or even three times, our size.

When I presented the opportunity, it was shot down quickly, so quickly I was stunned into silence. In the end we went ahead with the event after some finagling. It turned out to be the largest event in the history of the college and netted the library nearly $20,000 in one night. On paper, it did not seem the right thing to do, but the risk of doing it did. Of course you cannot count on success every time, but every year we had the event, I knew we would be more than successful, that being defined by making money rather than breaking even. And we were, for six years straight. Only taking a risk will yield such positive returns but you need to be aware that it can also yield the opposite. (Had we lost money would my contract have been renewed? I doubt it, but that is what risk-taking means.)

Seventh, make your plans comprehensible to your clientele. When communicating with members, make sure they understand you and what you're doing. This means avoiding library-speak. *Some* jargon ultimately will be necessary to convey your story. But if you are going to be successful in getting your message across, it will be necessary to eliminate jargon, avoid the jillion abbreviations common in our library parlance, and translating everything else to a language everyone can understand.[22] So, for example, talking about *periodicals* and *serials* as separate entities (the way most librarians do) may not really be the best way to go. You make have to simplify everything and talk about *magazines*. A good rule of thumb is to take what you have written and give it to someone completely unfamiliar to libraries and their operations and see how many things they do not understand. Strive for brevity, and clarity.[23]

Do not forget partnerships in communicating your group value.[24] It may be that you can team up with another friends group, or with other entities within your organization to increase your impact and effectiveness. This must be handled carefully because you do not want to confuse your audience. If you are small, however, it may be the only way you can get a hearing at all. Partnering with a group you know as much about as you can should go without saying.

Finally, notice should be given, regarding face-to-face communications, which will be treated separately in a later chapter. One *must* not soft-pedal this form of communication, which may well be the best form of all. For example, never underestimate the advantage of taking someone to lunch and talking about your goals. This can be anyone on the membership from the least likely supporter to your president or board chairperson. The chance to speak face-to-face far outdistances any other means for it is during the face-to-face encounters that you have the change to note inflection, read body language and ask questions regarding your successful communication.

There you have it. Just about every way possible you can communicate with your members and perhaps some new ways you have not considered. Although the Web cannot ever replace a full-service library, it can provide advantages that are unprecedented. Use them, and all the conventional means of communicating with your members to your fullest ability. Then sit back and reap the dividends.

> **AT A GLANCE**
>
> - Communicating with your members is the key to successful friends groups.
> - Your purpose should be to solicit funds and seek new members, but not at the expense of things like advocacy or volunteerism.
> - Communicating takes many forms, so don't rely on only one format.
> - Communication can be formal or informal; both are important.
> - Communication should be frequent, well-done, persuasive and varied.
> - Your official communications should strike a happy balance between frugality and extravagance; you don't want them too cheaply or too expensively executed.
> - Written correspondence should read well, be well-edited, and adhere to the standard rules of English.
> - Seek a "voice" that is distinctly your own.
> - Do some homework to see when your notices should go out. A little research can make the difference between your news or appeal being one of a hundred, or one of a handful.
> - Communicate through e-mails, listserves, websites, blogs, e-zines and newsletters.
> - Don't forget to use the more formal means of communication as well: dinners, luncheons, special mailings.
> - Think big, whether or not your membership is there yet. Look for ways to broaden your base by broadening the reach of your communiques.

ENDNOTES

1. R.M. Losee, "Communication Defined as Complementary Informative Processes," *Journal of Information, Communication and Library Science* 5, no. 3 (March 1999): 1. This is an otherwise useful article but its ponderousness often crushes its meaning. In other words, it may fail parts, of all, of the communication test.

2. M.Y. Herring, "'The Times They Are A-Changin'—But Are We?" *Library Journal* 126, no. 17 (October 15, 2001): 42–45. The article was featured as a cover story. We also later issued a white paper on same, which is on our Web site at www.winthrop.edu/dacus.

3. G.R. Miller, "On Being Persuaded: Some Basic Distinctions," in *Persuasion: New Directions in Theory and Research*, ed. M.E. Roloff and G.R. Miller (Beverly Hills, CA: Sage, 1980), 11–28. Quoted in James B. Stiff, *Persuasive Communication* (New York: The Guilford Press, 1994), 4.

4. K.B. Borei, "The Reward of Managing an Electronic Mailing List," *Library Trends* 47, no. 4 (Spring 1999): 86.

5. "Making a List." *PC Magazine* (May 21 2002): 4 pages.

6. If you think the "ranters" aren't much to worry about, think again. More than one listserv has been shut down, or taken off-line, because often disagreeable people boorishly insist on dominating the discussion with offbeat, inappropriate or irrelevant messages.

7. "Making a List." PC Magazine, (May 21 2002), 4 pages.

8. Ibid.

9. Ibid.

10. Blogs are legion in number now. Some of the better ones are http://little-greenfootballs.com/weblog or www.marginalrevolution.com. Both are political in nature.

11. A.W. Boykin and A. Kross, "Creating Library Newsletters on the World Wide Web," *Virginia Libraries* 45, no. 2 (April/June 1999): 14.

12. M. Seadle, "Libraries as Publishers," *Library High Tech* 16, no. 2 (1998): 5, 18.

13. Ibid.

14. Ibid., 248.

15. Ibid. 250.

16. W. Arant and C. Clark, "Academic Library Public Relations: An Evangelical Approach," *Library Administration and Management* 13, no. 2 (Spring 1999): 90–95.

17. Ibid., 90.

18. A good case in point is Jan Hendrik Schon who was fired by Bell Laboratories for fraudulent and fabricated information. Of the seventeen articles now in question, all are still on the Web and a search by nearly all search engines will produce those "groundbreaking" results in physics will never mentioning his firing. See *Wired News* (September 25, 2002), at www.wired.com/news/technology/0,1282,55391,00.html.

19. See, for example, C. Kennerdale, "Advertising through Newsletters and E-mail," *EContent* (June 2001): 52–53.

20. Ibid., 52.

21. These have been adapted for this purpose from T. Kirchner, "Advocacy 101 for Academic Librarians," *College and Research Libraries News* 60, no. 10 (November 1999): 845. Kirchner quotes E.E. Bingham, "Library Advocacy," *LLA Bulletin* 58 (Fall 1995): 86. It goes without saying that these rules apply to all libraries, not just academic ones.

22. A brief but very helpful piece is by D.C. Cramer, "How to Speak Patron," *Public Libraries* 37, no. 6 (November/December 1998). Cramer specifically writes about patron-librarian encounters but the article has wider application here.

23. See M. Gordon, "Newsletters That Work, Part 2: Content and Impact," *College and Research Libraries News* 1 (January 1997): 8–9.

24. P. Mileham, J. Rulle, and S.S. Berry, "Playing Well With Others: Increasing Your Library-Campus Partnerships," *Collection Management* 26, no. 3 (2001): 77–86.

7 MAXIMIZING ADVOCACY AND SUPPORT

For much of this book, friends-raising and fund-raising have been the premeditated focus. Given the time constraints that friends groups and other fund-raising ventures require, it is highly unlikely that: a) the group would have members who have time to devote to fund-raising, as well as additional time to devote to advocacy; and, b) that the financial pressures would ameliorate to the degree that advocacy groups would be preferable to time spent trying to raise funds.

Do not get me wrong. Advocacy is fundamental to any library. In point of fact, every member of every friends group is involved in advocacy. Advocacy is *essential to any type of friends group*. Whether you are trying to convince the trustees of your public library that a new addition is necessary, and then later the community in a bond bill, or your board of trustees that a thirteen percent increase in periodicals is not hyperbole, you are engaged in some form of advocacy. *Any attempt to convince others of the importance of what goes on at the library you represent is advocacy*. A separate chapter on the same may seem redundant since it is so fundamentally an important part of the warp and woof of friends groups.

Advocacy can, however, be an end in itself, just like fund-raising, and for many public libraries it is as preeminent as fund-raising. Often advocacy is stressed as the primary initiative. Two other separate imbroglios arise in libraries, creating the necessity of an advocacy-only group, and hence the need for a chapter on this separate topic.

> Advocacy is *essential in any type of friends group*... if only to convince city budget planners not to limit library budgets to the point of impotence.

MONEY ISN'T EVERYTHING

First, there are the numerous public libraries that *must* seek some sort of advocacy if only to convince city budget planners not to limit library budgets to the point of impotence. It should go without saying that there are also many state-supported, academic libraries that also fall into this category owing to state budget shortfalls across the country.[1] Second, some private colleges and universities prohibit any fund-raising outside the office of development, or its facsimile.[2] For all these institutions there remain only advocacy-type friends groups. They may

> You can have advocacy without fund-raising, but you cannot have fund-raising without advocacy.

be thought of as groups that plow the ground for fund-raising to be done by others. Think of advocacy as library support by other means. *You can have advocacy without fund-raising, but you cannot have fund-raising without advocacy.*

So what is advocacy? Library advocacy is persuading the public interest about libraries, and about all they do for democracy, including and providing for the means of a well-informed electorate.[3] In other words, it amounts to reminding the public that libraries are valuable for their resources, of course, but they are also quite valuable for their preservation, strengthening, and encouraging of democracy. With that in mind, let us explore advocacy more fully.

ADVOCACY IN LIEU OF FUND-RAISING

If fund-raising *per se* is difficult for library friends groups, library advocacy groups may be harder still. It is easy to see why. With fund-raising groups there is at least the hope, however faint, that the group can actually realize some of the very concrete goals it sets. Suppose the friends group sets ten thousand dollars as a goal to raise for the library. It is easy to see when that type of goal is reached.

With advocacy groups, defining success may be more elusive. In the case of a public library friends group, advocating the passage of a bond or millage is of course known when it passes. On the other hand, instilling an appreciation, creating an awareness, understanding and appreciating the value of libraries—all legitimate goals of advocacy groups—may be less easy to see when achieved, whether the target audience is in the general public or a given state legislature.

Academic institutions have much to learn about advocacy from their public library counterparts.[4] Public libraries have used advocacy groups to great effect on questions that come before the electorate. Having an *active* advocacy group in place can become particularly important as various needs arise at different times. If a new wing of the public library is needed, the friends advocacy group will be instrumental in making the case to do it, even if the friends group never directly raises one dollar. Such groups are not only effective in making the case outside the library's immediate sphere of influence, but *inside* it as well. Advocacy groups can be the catalyst that galvanizes public sentiment in favor of a given need.

ADVOCACY GROUPS: CARE AND USE

Advocacy groups are structured in much the same way as friends groups. The main difference is that there is no need for an ongoing program committee that might present various events that would otherwise draw scarce funds for a venture not immediately obvious to outsiders. This does not mean that such groups *never* put on programs. They might well put on programs to highlight the need for a particular goal, or simply "to tell the story" of the library to any who will listen. Obviously fund-raising friends groups do the same, the only difference being that those groups will then ask for the funding. Advocacy groups, on the other hand, will focus on making the case and why, without asking for funds outright.

HOW ADVOCACY GROUPS WORK WITH LIBRARIES

Let us suppose that a public library administration determines through a feasibility study that the library needs new equipment. All the internal members are on board, and the advocacy group is in place. Now what?

The advocacy group and the library administration come together and the library staff outlines the need for this new equipment, the number and purpose and value or advantages of it, the overall cost, and so forth. Then a brainstorming session follows on who or what the roadblocks might be—taxes too high, bond bills, under-served populations, and so on. Following this would be discussions about how this might be presented: commercials (radio, television) ads, flyers, presentations to targeted groups, and more. Then key players might be discussed and a campaign developed. Is a march on city hall in order? Do you have a "read-in" or try something dramatic, such as, What would it be like if the library vanished tomorrow, and so on. From this point, it is up to the advocacy group to "take over" and execute the plan. This is not prescriptive but suggestive. This small blueprint should provide a small insight on how an advocacy group might proceed.

Of course equipment is not the only goal. Advocacy groups might serve as focus groups for a particular need by providing information to a larger public on why that need is essential.[5] They might call in certain parts of the library's clientele, and use a questionnaire or survey to find out if such a goal is needed and why. They might outline why a new building, or a new addition, is required. Because such groups are voluntary in nature, the issue of providing funding for such groups is moot. They should know ahead of time that the outreach effort is for the library alone and no additional funds will be made available. This requirement limits the effectiveness of such groups only because it is hard to sustain a voluntary effort over a long period of time.

KINDS OF ADVOCACY GROUPS

Advocacy groups can be used in a number of ways, any one of which might prove just the difference between gaining acceptance of a particular need, or losing it altogether. These might be grouped as *goal-driven*, *legislative*, and *needs-based*. These divisions are somewhat artificial since each group's work overlaps into both the other areas. For the sake of discussion, however, the delineation proves useful.

Goal-Driven Advocacy Groups. Such groups may be formed at various times for particular needs. For example, the library may be without an endowment fund for books. Unfortunately this is not altogether unusual among libraries that number 400,000 or fewer books. Larger institutions will most likely already have endowments in place. Even for libraries that have endowments, the endowments may be too small for the library to realize any real gains (during these financial times, even a $100,000 endowment will yield *less than* five thousand dollars annually). Oftentimes, unless the endowment exceeds half a million dollars, it is likely that the library is not realizing enough to make a significant difference during budget recisions. Consequently, efforts to raise the endowment are in order. If the library cannot work though a friends group *per se* to acquire the funding, the advocacy group is still an option.

Such a group could be made up of individuals both on and off campus (academic), in and out of the library (public or special). They could be organized and charged with explaining why such an endowment for the library is required. This could range from budget-relieving (better than nothing) to budget-enhancing (much more desirable).

Having a group that will make the library's case for it is far superior to having the dean or director of the library make it. The reasons are obvious: such a group does not have what would constitute a conflict of interest, or at least what could be viewed as one. It does not matter that the information the group gathers might come directly from the library administration's own research. It is far superior and more highly effective to have a group present the needs on behalf of the library itself.

Experience teaches that when friends groups go about what might be called the "discovery" portion on a given issue, they are far more convinced, and more convincing, than groups that are spoon-fed all they advocate. The distance from the dean or director's office, and the group itself, is all the more helpful in the process as the impression is that this is a recognizable need, not one internally generated.

Once again, selection of members is obviously critical. It cannot be just anyone. If truth be told, *some* library users willing to "make a case for the library" may not themselves be the right ones for a given

---

TIP: Create the right advocacy groups for the right task

- Goal-Driven Advocacy Groups
- Legislative Advocacy
- Needs-based Advocacy

advocacy project. Whether owing to eccentricities or some other reason, *some* library users, even sincere and quite generous ones, may not be the best fit for the advocacy task. Choosing which members takes skill and investigation.

CHOOSING THE RIGHT ADVOCATES

> Choose advocates who have high credibility, who are well-respected and articulate, and who are willing to research an issue.

First, choose those who are articulate and well respected within the community. Second, choose those who have high credibility. The library advocate who each month, or worse, each week, sounds off in the letters to the editor may not be the best choice. While they may be ardent, they may also spell trouble for the library. Third, choose those whose research about the issues is impeccable. This can only be done if *you* or your designate, examines the materials that will be used to make the case. If for any reason you or your designate finds the material lacking, you *must* not choose that person, or all allow that information to go forward. If it cannot convince you, it *will not* convince anyone else.

If your library is an academic one, look for faculty who are respected members of their discipline *and* the community. One mistake library directors can easily make is to choose a faculty member who is widely respected by students. Eight out of ten times, you will be right on the money. But those two out of ten may spell disaster for you. *Do your homework* and make sure that the faculty member chosen has not incited the chair of the board of trustees to distraction, or worse, flunked (whether rightly or wrongly, it doesn't matter) a trustee's son, daughter, or favorite relative. Moreover, make sure that he or she has the community's ear. University campuses are filled to overflowing with colorful characters, some of whom may not yet have reached maturity. Choosing the "campus radical" who is much beloved on campus but loathed off campus is the exactly the wrong mix.

If your library is a public one, members chosen should be those in good standing with the community. Most likely these will be influential business men and women, and/or politicians. If the latter, so much the better. Obviously garnering the help of city council members or other important figures might be the difference between success and failure.

Legislative Advocacy. Public, special, and academic libraries (especially state-supported ones) can benefit from this sort of advocacy. A public library may need to increase its annual budget, or may be looking at millage issues for a larger budget share. An academic library may be considering a new library building, or a new addition.

The local special library may need help in buying land for expansion, or help in securing more funds for a special exhibit or special purchase.

Whatever the reason, again *choice of members is critical for success*. Members chosen for the first type of group may *not* be helpful in this group. Members chosen for this group must be chosen for their political clout. It does not matter whether the political clout is of one party or another, *so long as the person chosen is not of the opposite political party to which he or she must make the pitch*. This underscores a rather obvious point: libraries by necessity *must* remain nonpartisan on most issues, however difficult that may be.

Some will doubtless complain that one party is more amenable to library support than the other. Obviously local politics obtain here, but it is a sure death warrant the group signs when the advocate is overtly partisan. This is especially true of *academic* libraries. Most academic librarians gravitate to one-party politics by nature of being academics.[6] But this will eventually catch up with them when the opposite party takes over both state houses and/or the governorship. Then what?

Choose members for this group who are honest and above-board. Watch out for political-wannabees. The *last* thing you want on your hands is someone whose agenda is not your own, but who uses your political clout to service or advance theirs. Once discovered—and they will be regardless of how smooth or slick they are, or think they are—your case will be destroyed and your credibility leveled.

Careful planning, and the right people in the right place at the right time can garner for your group every goal it sets. Studying your potential members will make the difference here. In addition to looking for the honest face, you also need to find an articulate voice. *Someone* will have to make the case and while in many instances it will be the dean or director, there are those off-times in which it will be necessary for you protege or proxy to make the case. If you have done your homework well, you should have a person or persons who can undertake this task easily and well.

Much of this discussion about legislative advocacy has centered around the idea of certain items: equipment, book collections, buildings. But don't sell short the advocacy group that will make the *idea* of libraries a regular feature of their conversations. Just having someone who is always speaking well about libraries to others, who is also highlighting their advantages and underscoring their strengths will speak volumes later. In many ways, this is the ideal approach, for what legislator who has been fed a steady diet of "libraries are our intellectual and cultural lifeblood" spiel, could ever turn down a given increase of whatever kind for the library in his or her district?

General advocacy helps every cultural unit from libraries to museums to other community cultural icons. It will not matter that your library is lumped in with dozens of others at a given point in time. What will matter is when your particular issue arises and no one seems to be able to articulate what it is or why anyone would want it. General legislative advocacy is never wasted "air time" by any stretch of the imagination. When your "moment in the sun" comes up, you will be ready to draw upon the good capital that has been distributed by your group long before you arrive.

Needs-based Advocacy. Needs-based advocacy groups are groups that have as their agenda, their *raison d'être*, items which the library has identified as essential. What the advocacy group does in this case is collect data and distribute it in a fashion that will say to the audience, "this is what is needed and this is how you can help us get it." Needs-based advocacy groups are not necessarily groups that advocate needs only in front of an audience who can pay for the needs. It may be a group that speaks to civic clubs about the public library in general, or a group of faculty who praise the values of the academic library.

Also, do not forget the uses to which you can put what you've learned while publicizing your advocacy. Advocacy is often a matter of sharing information and the more you share, and the more often you share it, the greater the chances your group has of making its case heard. For example, your group could send out e-mails and post flyers in key areas. One obvious place for the flyers is the library, of course, but that's only the beginning. With careful planning of your flyers, you could create a small groundswell in your favor.

Suppose the group decides that wireless laptops are needed. A needs-based advocacy group could distribute flyers in various areas of the city that read, "Imagine Doing Research Anywhere You Want! Even Here. Ask for Wireless Access." Placing these in restaurants, public centers and elsewhere will plant the seeds you need to "grow" your case.

Student groups have enormous influence on most campuses. Why friends groups at academic institutions do not make more use of them remains a mystery, at least until recently. Over the last three years, many student governments organizations—the standard SGAs familiar to anyone who has been to college in the last fifty years—have fallen by the wayside owing to lack of interest, capable leadership or the rise of the number of students working full time. Even with this change there remain large numbers of loosely coupled student groups that friends advocacy groups could draw upon to make their case heard.

Levels of advocacy might be broken down in the following manner:

- Regional Support[7]
- Community
- Administration (funding source)
- Natural Allies

Distinguish the levels of advocacy

- Regional Support
- Community
- Administration (funding source)
- Natural Allies

Regional Support. This is defined by however your group defines it. It can be as small as your library's circulation area or as large as your state. Whichever it is, you'll want to take into account the audience you are trying to reach and tell your story. A large public library might want to think in these terms, while a large academic facility will think even larger. When advocating library needs over a large region it will be necessary to keep the message simple and general.

Community. Generally the locale is the area in which the library is located and does most of its business. Public libraries are far more likely to be doing this kind of advocacy than academic ones, but there is no reason why the latter should not be doing this as well. Advertizing what you do in the community can be as simple as having groups showcase what the library does, to placing articles in the local paper and through other community groups. Advocacy through community groups—all of them regardless of size—is especially effective.

There remain the professional groups still to descry: attorney groups, physicians, realtors and the like. These groups should not be overlooked but do not get your hopes up to high. Not only are they hard to break into, but on the whole they are not very responsive groups to anything that does not advance that group's predetermined goals.

If the dean or director is not going to be making these presentations, it is highly advisable to audition those who do. You want someone who can deliver a *brief*, hard-hitting talk that mixes information with humor. The talk should never exceed twenty minutes and always allow for a question and answer period. If you don't audition these talks you may short-circuit the effectiveness.

Administration. While the dean or director will be making this case during budget hearings, we all know that this case, no matter how well it is made, is not always as successful as one hopes. Having others help to make this case throughout the year to add to your own case can only help when the budget hearings are finally held. Of course you will want to make certain that you and your advocacy group are making the same case, and this can only be done with careful planning. What you stress in January may not be what is needed in August, so the need to fine tune presentations throughout the year will be necessary.

Ferreting out those who can help you—Academic Vice President, Faculty Senate Chairperson, Chamber president, mayor or vice mayor, or others—it's critical that you make some contact with these members so you can have your voice heard. How often this is ignored in libraries—more often academic ones than public—is surprising. If you are not already on the president's schedule of annual meetings, make a date to be on it this year. It is the only way to be sure that your needs will be examined carefully. Using a combination of approaches will make certain that when you do make your case to whatever budget board you must, it *will not be—it cannot be—the first time your voice is heard, or the first time this need is aired.*

One other group that comes to mind, which could as easily be placed in this category as in the former, is your legislature. There is every reason why you need to get to know these individuals and, equally important, for them to get to know you. The first thing you need to do is visit your legislators. Whoever represents your district, and however many of them there are, be sure you call upon them from time to time.[8] Invite them to lunch or dinner and above all, invite them to your library. Be sure they are on mailing lists of various kinds and are aware that you are doing good work in the community.

Natural Allies. For public or special libraries, or academic libraries, natural allies will differ. What you will have to do is find out who these are and began the process of cultivation to make them a part of your advocacy group. For example, in a public setting, it may be the newly elected Chamber member, or a new state or congressional representative for the area. You may need an advocate for a special project, a new building or some one-time purchase. In a special setting, it may be a new board of trustees, or one who has served for a long time on that board that you'll use for a special purpose. It may even be a minister or some important civic official in your town. In an academic setting it will likely be a faculty member, but not just any faculty member, as warned about above. All of these are good reasons to have in place a strong advocacy group who will make these cases along with you when you go before whatever budget authority you must address to secure them.

The more you work at it, the more likely you will eventually hit upon the right "voice" to bring the choir into full chorus. If you've done your homework, you shouldn't have any trouble galvanizing discussion, people, and resources to the resolution of your library's current entanglement. As Gail Bush relates, "Think holistically...[S]trive to bring together innovative programs that impact the entire [institution] and bring it together as a single learning community."[9]

THE MEDIA IS THE MESSAGE!

Do not forget radio and public service television programs. Be sure you are on your organization's publicity list so you can be called about things that come up regarding your library or the profession at large. The local talk radio in your area may be a perfect avenue for making your group's voice heard, and the library's, too. Call them even when you're not on and try to get an appropriate word in edgewise about the library. Talk with student and alumni groups, write letters to the editor and identify and then meet with as many important and influential (and even marginally influential) individuals as you can. Always be reminding yourself: "If I think it's important to say once, I need to say it one hundred times."

Advocacy is also extremely helpful in putting an end to the librarian's age-old lament of, "No one really knows what we do." Whether it is the community at large in your public library, the constituents you serve in a special library setting, or your students, faculty and staff, advocacy groups are particularly useful in bringing the light to bear on getting the word out. It is important to remember, however, that they know not because you have not educated them well enough. Bush and Kwielford call this "awareness," but it can be called just about anything: education, publicity, information. Whatever you want to call it does not matter. What does matter is that you have a vehicle at the ready to tell people, tell them again and then after you've told them, remind them once more that you are doing certain things, and that what you do is exceedingly important.

PUBLIC LIBRARY ADVOCACY GROUPS CRITICAL

For public libraries, advocacy groups may be as equally important to the fund-raising arm as their friends groups. Since much of what public libraries are able to get in terms of funding is based upon various kinds of votes, telling the public your story is essential.[10] If you can arrange your fund-raising arm to be your advocacy arm as well, so much the better. For example, at some point during the year, amid your fund-raising jeremiads, you could present what the library does for the community as a public service. Provide a day where patrons who come into the building to learn about the library. A display indicating "Where Your Money Goes" might be particularly effective. A flyer that announces the ten best things that can happen at the library might be the very thing your group could hand out at the local grocery and department stores while your circulation folks place one in each book checked out.

Bookmarks with a few "library tidbits" bulleted down the center are very effective ways of saying what you do and why. If your budget allows for it, an appreciation dinner for advocates is also well worth the effort. The point is, like everything we do in libraries, there is a right and a wrong way to do it. It is easy to remember which is the wrong way: doing nothing and hoping for the best. If you are not making the case, or providing data so someone else can, then who will? If not you, who? If not now, when?

LIBRARY ADVOCACY NOW!

Is advocacy another name for special interest pleading? Hardly. Remember that library advocacy is advocacy for the public interest, for all that is good in democracy.[11] But in order to "get there" it will require large numbers of friends groups making the case for libraries one at a time. ALA's Library Advocacy Now! (LAN) can provide important training in this regard, and any advocacy group should not fail to examine this option. As Patricia Schuman, past ALA president and leading library advocate, points out the goal is to help establish a nationwide group of advocates ready to make the case for libraries wherever they are.[12] Library Advocacy Now! can help train your group to be more effective at what it does, and how it goes about doing it.[13] Add this to FOLUSA, mentioned earlier, and your library advocacy group will be well underway to achieving what is required to do what it is you need doing.

> ALA's Library Advocacy Now! (LAN) can provide important training. Go to www.ala.org and click on Issues and Advocacy.

LIBRARIES FOR THE FUTURE

Libraries for the Future also exists to help raise awareness about libraries and their needs.[14] The group has a listserv (PUB-ADV), a Web site (www.lff.org), and more than eight thousand advocates. While Libraries for Future is more public-library oriented, academic libraries should understand that the illumination is the same: making libraries important enough to rest on the front burner (in many cases *getting on* the burner at all is a major feat). Be ready to learn from whatever the source, whatever the slant. If it moves the library forward, you can bet it's something you need to examine.

HEAVENLY MARRIAGE: LIBRARY ADVOCACY AND FRIENDS GROUPS

Library advocacy is, of course, something done by every friends group. If your friends group is not advocating your library and your library's services, it is missing a key ingredient. But library advocacy groups, even without the fund-raising element added, can still reap numerous library benefits. If you don't start one, you'll never know. And once you do, who knows what bountiful harvest awaits you?

> ### AT A GLANCE
>
> - Advocacy groups are critically important.
> - Although most of this book has been about fund-raising, advocacy is equally important.
> - Some libraries, for various reasons, cannot raise funds. For them, there remains only the advocacy group.
> - Advocacy groups, like friends groups that raise funds, need care and cultivation.
> - Advocacy groups and the library administration can work hand-in-glove to achieve great things.
> - There are several kinds of advocacy groups, and while the division is somewhat artificial, it is helpful to deliniate them.
> - The three types of advocacy groups are: goal-driven, legislative, and needs-based.
> - All advocacy groups require care in selecting their members.
> - Levels of advocacy are: regional, community, administrative and natural allies.
> - Advocacy groups rely heavily on media. Be certain that your message is clear, concise and powerful.
> - ALA's Library Advocacy Now! is a most helpful organization, as is Libraries for the Future.

ENDNOTES

1. See for example any state-by-state budget round-up in *The Chronicle of Higher Education*, generally the fall issue. As of February 2003, fifty out of fifty states have budget shortfalls so severe that higher education budgets will be reduced to meet the difference.
2. Oftentimes these are private, church-related institutions.
3. See P.G. Schuman's excellent article, "Speaking Up and Speaking Out: Ensuring Equity through Access," *American Libraries* 30, no. 9 (October 1999): 50–56. Also, L. Kniffel, "Power and Influence," (Interview with Schuman.) *American Libraries* 27, no. 8 (September 1999): 52–55. See also C. Watkins, "Chapter Report: Library Advocacy—A Local Brew with National Ingredients," *American Libraries* 27, no. 11 (December 1996): 9.

4. J.M. Zahuha and L. Wycoff, "Academic Libraries Enriched by Friends," *PNLA Quarterly* 64, no. 3 (Spring 2000).

5. See D.W. Johnson, "Focus Groups," in *The Tell-It! Manual* (American Library Association (Chicago: ALA, 1996), 176–87. The sample interviews to be used with this method (focus groups) are particularly helpful.

6. This point has been confirmed repeatedly by the work of P. Lazaerfeld, S.M. Lipsett, and the Richters.

7. See G. Bush and M.A. Kwielford, "Advocacy in Action," *Teacher Librarian* 28, no. 5 (June 2001). Available at www.teacherlibrarian.com/tlmag/v_28/v_28_5_feature.html.

8. It's always a good idea to be sure to pass this through you own chain of command. In academic settings, for example, presidents generally like to be the main (if not the only) legislative contact on campus. This makes excellent sense since an issue may come up that you might think has nothing to do with your institution (and you certainly know has nothing to do with your library) only to discover later that it is tied to some performance funding issue, or some other matter that will affect your institution adversely.

9. Bush and Kwielford, 10.

10. D. Debowski, "The Funding Game: Rules for Public Library Advocacy," *The Australian Library Journal* 49, no. 2 (May 2000): 189.

11. See P.G. Schuman's excellent article, "Speaking Up and Speaking Out: Ensuring Equity through Access," *American Libraries* 30, no. 9 (October 1999):50–56. Also, L. Kniffel, "Power and Influence," (Interview with Schuman.) *American Libraries* 27, no. 8 (September 1999): 52–55. See also, C. Watkins, "Chapter Report: Library Advocacy—A Local Brew with National Ingredients," *American Libraries* 27, no. 11 (December 1996): 9.

12. Ibid., 51.

13. A video recording exists and can be used for this purpose, *Library Advocacy Now!* (ALA Video/Library Video Network, 1997); 23 minutes, $99. This may be the perfect thing you need to do to get your group moving in the right direction, followed up by another kind of training offered by ALA.

14. B. Goldberg, "Unleashing Patron Power at Libraries for the Future," *American Libraries* 28, no. 5 (May 1997): 57–59.

8 PROGRAMMING A FRIENDS EVENT

You will discover soon enough the necessity of having *some* electrifying major friends group event that will rivet attention to your program. The purpose of the event may be to bring in money. It may be to showcase your group, as if to say, "We're here and we need you to join us to do this wonderful thing." If your group is devoted strictly to advocacy, it may be an event that would highlight in a significant manner some main purpose: a millage, a bond bill, or legislation before your state lawmakers. It might be an event just to showcase library services. No matter what your type group, you will always need some annual event (biannual or monthly) to bring in additional members, a friends-making event if you will.

The purpose does not determine the kind of event you have. Nearly any kind of event will work for any of these purposes. What you have to remember is that all of these events will cost money. If you are not going to charge, then some way of recouping your costs—and there will be some—must be considered. For example, if you are not raising funds but creating awareness, perhaps you can find three or four sponsors to underwrite your event. In every case, however, you will need a budget, about which more later. This chapter is written from the perspective of an event for fund-raising purposes.

THE BIG SHOW

> When just about any local outreach that relies at all on private funding needs to supplement its budget, the organization holds an event. Likewise, it is very nearly impossible to have a successful friends group without also having *some* sort of activity that will bring people together and raise funds.

When just about any local outreach that relies at all on private funding needs to supplement its budget, the organization holds an event. The local elementary school sells raffle tickets. Your church or temple holds a bake sale, and your favorite charity washes cars or sells Christmas paper. Public radio holds biannual fund-raising appeals. Even politicians who are awash in money still hold various dinners at an incredible one thousand dollars a plate, and hundreds, even thousands turn out. Likewise, it is very nearly impossible to have a successful friends group without also having *some* sort of activity that will bring people together and raise funds (or other purposes as stated above). Of the $160 billion donated annually to various charitable causes, eighty-eight percent comes from private individuals. Only the remaining twelve percent comes from foundations and corporations.[1] While some might argue that this is not true of publicly funded institutions, I beg to differ. If "State University" does not locate some major donor, *something* at state will not get done: the new library building, the sports arena, the so-and-so endowment fund, and so on. So, what sort of event do you need to stage? Your imagination is the limit. To spark your thinking, here are some examples.

At the Friends of the Neill Public Library and the Friends of the Whitman County Library, an annual Lentil Festival catches the attention. Yes, you read that right, *Lentil* Festival. As a vegetarian for some fifteen years, I can attest to the delight of lentils but I imagine some readers may be puzzled.[2] The two libraries combine for over four hundred gallons of lentil chili, and five thousand people come out to attend hundreds of activities.[3]

More commonplace is what happened at the Friends of the Library in Ponte Vedra Beach, Florida, where "Adventures in Wonderland" included a four-day fund-raising event that culminated in a black-tie gala affair, wine tasting and a shopping bazaar. Each event required a donation or purchase (two hundred fifty dollars, eighty dollars, and free, respectively) and cost the library only about one thousand three hundred dollars to publicize. For that investment, the event garnered seventy-five thousand dollars.[4] It is instructive to see that the Ponte Verdra Beach Friends did not rely on one event alone, but on a combination of events lasting more than one day.

The Medford Public Library Friends program offers nearly a dozen passes to local points of interest in Boston. To get the passes you have to be a "Minuteman" library cardholder.[5] The Friends of the Library of Collier County, Florida, another public library, offers a number of ways to attract attention, one of which is their now fabled "Classic Film Festival." The film festival is a widely followed event. Each season commentary is offered by a local film expert, and the library's Web page offers various bits of information for users who may be taking part. Some films are offered on more than one night.

Of course these (and the dozens mentioned in the first chapter) are only some of the many ways that you can use to bring people together. The question remains: what are the important components to putting on an annual event with one part or three dozen?

COMPONENTS OF THE BIG SHOW

The elements are essentially the same whether you are staging a colossal annual dinner with a nationally-known novelist, or a fun-run for your town of two thousand. It does not matter whether you are hosting a luncheon, a bake sale, wine tasting, or an auction. Whatever it is you decide to do, you will have to take a number of issues into account. These are, in no particular order:

- Deciding on the Event
- Time of the Event
- Location of the Event
- Theme of the Event
- Publicity for the Event
- Press Connections
- Researching the Event

Several of these points will have subpoints of departure, but for nearly any large annual event meant to galvanize your group, these seven rubrics will have to be addressed in some way. Some groups may tackle them with seven subcommittees (or their equivalent), while others may want the executive director to ride shotgun on each one. It really comes down to determining the quality of your group and placing it in the hands of those who will not drop the ball (and then watching them to be sure they don't). If you cannot be sure, then you, or your designee, will have to take up the slack. In the movie *A League of Their Own*, Tom Hanks tells Madonna, "There's no crying in baseball!" Likewise, when planning friends events, there is no such thing as delegating everything, so you have only one thing to do.[6] Sure, you make assignments. But you must also be present to be sure these things you issue as edicts do in fact come to pass.

DECIDING ON THE EVENT

How do you go about deciding between a nationally known speaker or holding an auction; between a bake sale and a marathon? There is no silver bullet that allows you to make a failsafe decision but there are some things you should keep in mind.

1. Know Your Community. You cannot decide what to do unless you know what your community is like, as well as what it likes. If this is your first year in the community, you had better wait until the next year, or, best of all, until your third or fourth year. The reasons for this should be obvious. You cannot really know about where you live until you have *lived* there. You cannot possibly get to know all the "right" people in the community until you have been in that community and made your own contributions. Further, until you have lived in a place and gotten to know as many people as possible, you cannot make an educated guess about what will "fly" there. The biggest mistake you can make is to decide that what one library is doing is what you should do, or that what you did at your previous job is what you'll do at your present one.

It is also more than this. For example, you may live in a rural area where the average annual income is twenty-five thousand dollars. Will hosting an event for four hundred dollars a ticket work? You may be in an industrial area that has fallen on very bad times. Within a hundred miles of where I write this chapter there are towns that are literally going bankrupt owing to the collapse of textile mills from the success of NAFTA. Dozens and dozens of one hundred-year old companies have moved operations to Mexico and points north and south. A library seeking high-dollar affairs is destined to failure at these locales.

But do not be too quick to judge just by the cover of the book. Twenty years ago I gave a talk in the middle of coal country about beginning a friends group. The town had all the earmarks of a coal-mining community. I planned to keep the matter low key until my host gave me a tour of the city, including a wine store that regularly stocked five hundred dollar bottles of wine that routinely sold out.

2. Know the Other Stakeholders. Living in a community gives you a chance to know the other charitable organizations in the area, not the least of which will be other libraries, whether special, public or academic. What are these institutions doing, and what are all the other groups—civic and otherwise—already doing? Will you be duplicating their event and thus make yours an unlikely success? Worse, will you appear to be "horning in" on established events, or be viewed as a carpetbagger? Time is your only ally and you should court her to learn all that you can.

3. Know Your Budget? This may be a silly point, but really, is there *any* money to spend on this event and, if so, will it affect other spending lines? That is, does this event have its own independent line or will funds from this budget line be subtracted from others? This may sound sinister but unfortunately, as we pointed out in Chapter 1, library budgets are not the picture of salubrity these days.

You must know what is at your disposal and it is really not a bad idea (or even an exercise of bad faith) to *get in writing* what it is you have to spend. This does not have to sound as contractually formal as it may seem at first. A simple e-mail to your budget officer should clear this up. Even if you do not have any money to spend, taking a risk is not a bad idea, either. The first ever friends event with which I was involved had no money but we spent it anyway and brought in almost ten thousand dollars after expenses on our first dinner affair.

4. Finally, Know Your History. Has your group done this before and if so, how long ago? If this is a first run for your group (and if you work in academic setting chances are that it *is* the first time), what is

---

Select the best kind of BIG event by knowing your:

- Community
- Other Stakeholders
- Budget
- History

your staff like? Do you know them well? Are they willing to go the extra mile? While it may seem counterintuitive to everything else said heretofore, you really must take into account comments like, "That will never work here," or "We tried that and it didn't work." You can come off seeming ignorant of your own history, or simply too arrogant to be bothered by it. This is not to say, of course, that you should let these comments forestall you. You simply must take them into consideration and address them.

TIME OF THE EVENT

Most of what you learned under the history portion of the above question will aid you enormously in deciding *when* you want to host your event. First, what else is going on in your organization? Are there key events or programs that occur and have always occurred at the same time each year? For example, the city where I now live holds a citywide "Come See Me" event that occupies two weeks each April. We will not schedule any event then unless we are asked. If it is possible to piggyback on an event like this, then do so. Just be sure you do not appear to be an opportunist.

But you need to do even more. Check your "community calendar" for whatever events may coincide or even compete. For example, many cities host a "fall" event of some kind, focusing mostly on arts and crafts. Larger cites host even more widespread events, of course, and these you should be able to find out about through your Chamber of Commerce. Is the United Way revving up its annual campaign? Then wait until that event is over, or at the very least, until the kick off dinners are over. If you work in a public library, is the local college beginning or completing a city- or county-wide capital campaign? If so, wait a week or more before announcing yours.

What about the Red Cross, the Salvation Army and various other groups? You need to know so you can plan your event. What about church groups? Are their programs city- or county-wide? If so, hold off. Someone reading this may think, "If I do all that I'm sure to find there's no good time!" Quite possibly you will. But what you will also discover is that there are bad times and then there are positively horrid ones. You are really trying to find the time of the year that competes with the fewest number of other events. So, are you ready to schedule that event?

Not quite. You still need to think of a day of the week. Fridays and Sundays are generally very bad days. Wednesdays are also weak, but this is becoming increasingly less so. The remaining days of the week are generally fine so long as your event is not right in the middle of some sporting event, such as Monday Night Football, or some other

---

Consider and plan the BIG event:

- Time
- Location
- Publicity
- Press
- Research

time when half or more of your target audience will have a credible reason for not coming. It may be that if you decide on, say, a black tie affair, sporting events will not be as important. Bear in mind that giving half your targeted audience a ready-made reason for not coming will impede your level of success.

LOCALE OF THE EVENT

If any one part of planning a major event proves most difficult, the locale often is. When situating a business, location, location, location are the first three rules you need to remember; it is also the first *four* of a friends event. It is astonishing, but by and large, Americans do not like to go far from home; not even a few miles. One illustration should suffice.

Some years ago, I worked with a federal program designed to help displaced workers retool for other jobs. In a small southern town a computer giant had closed it doors. The employees made much more on average than anyone else in the city, in many cases two and three times as much as the average. When the company closed its large branch there, the federal program kicked in and we went to interview the laid off employees. To our astonishment, the employees set conditions on what jobs they would take. At the top of the list after "making as much or more that I was" stood "driving no more than five miles to work."

Given this inclination among many Americans, finding a centrally located place to host your event will take some thinking. You want to be sure there is ample parking. Our university president often says that we do not have a parking problem, we have a walking problem, and he's exactly right. Most people will not walk even half a mile. You also want to be sure that there is ample lighting in case the event is at night (but bear in mind those who do not or cannot drive at night), and that there is the proper amount of security. If no security is provided, you will have to hire it out. While it may be an added expense it will cost far less than a subsequent lawsuit over broken car mirrors and windows, or worse, bones. If you think such litigation is impossible, remember the woman who sued McDonald's for selling her hot coffee that *she* spilled in her lap.

Be sure your site is handicapped accessible. Not only is this considerate, it is also the law. Check ramps for the wheelchair bound, and be sure there is ample handicap-accessible parking. Do you have equipment or a signer for the hard of hearing? Is the site equipped for the off chance that someone will need medical care? All of these things are important and need to be taken into consideration. Check your library's (or organization's) liability insurance to see what you must require. Of course nothing could be easier than to have everything you need on site, but if this is an annual event, your onsite location must be large enough to accommodate most of those who want to come. Also be sure that all the speaking, presenting, or whatever it is you intend to do is available *and in working* condition.

THEME OF THE EVENT

Is this really important? All I can tell you is that in two decades of planning these events, not once have I hosted one where someone—a reporter, a ticket holder—did not call and ask what this was all about. It also helps if your event has "branding" recognition, as discussed earlier. You want folks to walk around town talking about this event. If there is some sort of verbal shorthand that allows for this, so much the better. For example, almost any memorable commercial has a tag line, a jingle, a catchphrase that allows others to associate the tag line with your event or organization. If you can capture this for your library you have secured at least a third of your publicity battle: definition.

You will want to have the theme of the event everywhere. During my involvement with our first friends event twenty years ago, we used that library's emblem as the theme, as mentioned earlier.[7] We also used Jefferson Cups, engraved with the name of our speaker and the date. These were stunning mementos of an event that most wanted to recall. You cannot imagine my pride when I would visit homes and see these cups proudly displayed on bookcases and other places.

All these things go into creating the right ambience about your event and its theme. It asserts your "presence" and forces others to take notice, who might not have otherwise. You will be surprise how important this ingredient is. And while the event may change from time to time, from a speaker one year, to a marathon the next, the theme—books, equipment, culture, whatever—should be easily recognizable as *your* group's event.

As mentioned earlier, this harkens back to the idea of branding, that which "create[s] a strong identity, a trustmark, a promise for you [group]."[8] This is important in order for you to give a personality to your group in the same way people know what Coke is, or recognize a Sprint commercial when they see one. You may think you do not have the money to do this but it does not take so much money as it does repeating the same thing over and over again. Even if the branding is as nebulous as "the Friends annual dinner affair," you have still identified an event with your group and made the publicity for that event so much easier the next time. If you are continuously successful, people will come to your event *regardless* of your speaker. It will be the fact of your event, not so much the notoriety of whatever or whoever is showcased at your event.

PUBLICITY FOR THE EVENT

I cannot over-stress how important it is to set aside money from your funds, however meager they may be—money for publicity. Publicity, especially for your kick-off event, is critical to your success. If libraries scrimp anywhere it is here and this is the *last* place you want to cut corners. You may want to review Chapter 5 on publicity and marketing. The event itself will suggest other areas on which you might want to concentrate or "target" your publicity.

This is a matter of promotion, which is nothing more than "Effectively putting [your] message across in the right place, at the right time, and to the right audience."[9] For example, you may decide that a marathon would be a good way to raise funds. You will want to be sure that all the civic clubs in your area are aware of the event, and may want to recruit some of them to work at yours. If you plan early enough—and of course you will—you will get notices in all their newsletters and magazines, if such are applicable. Furthermore, you will want to have notices posted at the YMCA and any other such "health clubs" as are in your area. If you are going to have tee shirts (and why not?) you surely will be able to find a sponsor for them by offering to place their name on the bottom. (If there are several clubs in your area you may have to do a program and put all of them on it if they are so inclined.) Of course you will also want to be sure to place publicity at every store that sells running shoes and apparel.

This is, of course, only one example. If you bring an author in, the same kind of thing can be done by focusing on bookstores, book clubs, and other similar groups. There are surely in your community small book groups of only a dozen or so members. Find them, and long before the event. In an increasing number of sizable cities (and some not so sizable) local newspapers are encouraging citywide book clubs where a given book is read by large numbers of people. Often these are local authors of some note, or new authors who have captured the attention of many. Can you get this author? So much the better for you will have an instant audience and a sizable amount of free publicity.

There really is no limit to the manner in which publicity can be done for these events. It merely requires planning and plenty of imagination. Of course no matter where you speak or your friends groups hold meetings, you will want to be sure that all the information about your event will be constantly before the public. All it takes is a tagline that merely repeats the particulars of the upcoming event. It should go without saying that your Web page and your library will be filled notices about it.

What about the publicity, *per se*? You should develop your publicity in an eye-appealing way. While professional help in this regard is ideal, it is not necessary. For example, you could give to your local art club or art students as a project. Recall that we gave our outreaches to the management classes at the university and they came up with a complete approach, including what to use as publicity. Remember to use all advertising avenues since you cannot always know where the right places are until you try them. That is, do not discount a possible outlet until you are certain it will not reach any of your clientele. Advertise on your Web page, as a byline on your e-mail, and through your friends group. Flyers are a particularly effective way if they are neat, grammatically correct, and easy to read. Desktop publishing, mentioned in an earlier chapter, provides an inexpensive way to be professional looking without the accompanying professional cost.

Your publicity should go everywhere, or as nearly everywhere as you can put it. In store windows, on cars in parking lots (with permission, of course) on conventional bulletins boards, as well as electronic ones. Local newspapers should provide enough free publicity (PSAs) for your event to get it before the public. But do not overlook alternative presses. By that I mean those free publications that are found in cafes, grocery stores, and elsewhere. (Of course some of these may not be appropriate, so be sure to read them before advertising in them.)

It is amazing what a little money can do for publicity, too. Friends groups that will not spend money on publicity will yield smaller returns in the long run. Poorly crafted newsletters and publicity will only end in embarrassment and friends events will be poorly attended. One group with which I had a loose association began spending a bit for publicity and saw its attended shoot up one hundred percent.

The point is that if you have something worth coming to, people will flock to it. But the *only* way they know that beforehand is through your publicity. If it is shoddy work, you can be sure that only the very faithful will be present.

PRESS CONNECTIONS

Press connections are not something you can "turn on" a few weeks before the event, and ignore after it. They have to be *cultivated*. Get to know the reporters in your area, especially those who cover events like the ones you will be hosting. The press can be a blessing and a curse, and on the same event. Although hard work and careful planning with the press went into every friends event with which I have been associated, astonishment at the coverage never ceased to amaze me. One event in particular stands out in my mind. Uncannily, I had been able to secure the speaking talents of a nationally and internationally known pundit. He had just come out with a new book, which was making the talk-show rounds, and his previous work had been one of those love-hate relationships with his readers. Either they loved him and bought everything, or they hated him viscerally and despised everything he ever wrote, but bought it all the same. Getting him to come to a very, very small library for an event that would take place in a town of less than twenty-five thousand proved more than a little difficult.

His name was instantly recognizable by all but the most benighted. I fully expected great press coverage and our group's press releases were dutifully printed everywhere they were sent. We had a capacity crowd, so much so that one week prior to the event we sold standing room only seats, followed by "foyer seating." This was a huge event for this small, rural town. As I made preparations to pick up my speaker—preparations that had themselves become something of a media event—a local reporter called and asked me, *"Could you swing by the paper and let us interview him before the dinner?"* I'm not sure now what I answered but the gist was no, but she would be welcomed at the press conference, along with the other reporters. To my utter amazement, coverage at the press conference included reporters from one hundred miles away, *but not our local reporter who worked less than one mile away*.

I relate this anecdote simply to underscore that you can, in fact, do everything right and it will still go wrong. Cultivate your press contacts early and often you will minimize the likelihood of such a ridiculous occurrence. By cultivation I mean calling them regularly (but not weekly), providing them with insights unrelated to your friends group, soliciting advice on press releases and studying style so you can supply them with stories that require little editing. It is not a bad idea to schedule a lunch biannually or even quarterly but you must be careful that this is not read as anything more than professional courtesy on your part.

For example, if you are new to an area it is not at all untoward to ask local reporters to lunch just to introduce yourself and your vision. These invitations would go beyond a general press conference as might be held upon your hiring. Regular updates (every four to six months) are also not out of the ordinary. This does two things. It establishes a *single* contact for the friends group. Reporters now have a ready contact for any number of library-related stories that may span the gamut of access to zoning, and copyright to Web-based research. Second, it also establishes an approachable individual ready to share accurate, dependable information. Reporters like nothing better than to have someone like this on hand upon whom they can call for quotes or background. If you really want to win big points, suggest stories that readers might find interesting. Reporters are rarely without ideas for stories but occasionally the news is slow and they are out of fresh ideas. Yours might be just the ticket to improve your coverage.

Having said all this, be prepared to read the story and find omissions, inaccuracies and outright misrepresentations. No reporter does this intentionally but since most work on deadlines—often deadlines that are measured by hours or minutes rather than days—it is too much to expect one hundred percent accuracy. Furthermore, even when a reporter does get a substantial lead time, day-to-day deadlines often prohibit double-checking each story. Do not get upset over this. When the omissions or errors are glaring, a polite call will help make sure the *next* story is better. Corrections and retractions may occur but even these are not always routine with every paper. The important point is to *remain calm*. This last thing you want to do is to be at odds with your local reporter or newspaper.

Should you provide exclusives? That depends on where you live. If your local news source is one of many in the immediate area, no. But if your news source is one of others that are some distance away, you probably should. You must live and work with your local press and providing them with material that they alone can have early will only strengthen the relationship.

RESEARCHING THE EVENT

Every event you do will become something of a mini-research project. It has to be for several reasons, the most obvious is that you will likely be asked about something and it makes you and your organization look good when you can be the authority. A less obvious reason has to do with details, in which we often find the devil of a mess. Our first friends group focused on authors. I also found it especially helpful to research the author thoroughly, looking for that small detail that will make his or her stay perfect. If your event does involve an author it should go without saying that you read his or her complete oeuvre, including the best critical texts. Of the six nationally known authors we hosted research about the speaker paid substantial dividends.

Even if your event is not a speaking affair but something else—an auction, silent or otherwise, a gala or something else—you will find the additional homework *always* pays off. And be sure you listen to, but do not rely upon exclusively, local input. During the production of a newsletter, years ago, I showcased a well-known woman in our community, who lived in one of the area's historic homes. One of our professors, a personal friend, told me about her, emphasized that I call upon her, and even provided many details. I used one of the harmless details he supplied in the newsletter and, much to my chagrin, ended up having to make a profuse apology. The detail was well known, but not one to her liking. I learned then that it was better to check and double check *everything* before going to press.

Another advantage is of course the press who will not have the time to examine in detail all that you will. Share your information liberally with all reporters. For example, you may want to create a fact sheet that provides dates and details about the event, the speaker and any interesting information that would make your event more enticing. If you are featuring an author, then a bibliography will certainly save your reporters much time and legwork. If you are tying into a historical event of local or national significance, the same is true. Suppose your event occurs in January. If applicable, you can tie the event to Martin Luther King Day. By doing so you will automatically generate more opportunities to advertise.

BUDGETING YOUR EXPENSES

You will want to budget for all this, and creating a budget worksheet is a good way to do that. The budget worksheet will do two things. First, it will help you keep your spending in check. Second, it will act as a checklist for all your event-related activities. It need not be complicated to be effective, and might look like this:

XYZ Wine Tasting

Overall Budget $5,000
Publicity
- Invitations—Printing (150) $125
- Invitations—Postage $55.50
- Brochures/Posters (Printing) $250
- Newsletters—Printing (680) $150
- Newsletters—Postage $250
- Miscellaneous $100

Rentals
- Site $100
- Sound System $150

Decorations $100
Wine
- Reds (6) $250
- Whites (6) $250

Hors d'ourves $300
Memorabilia
- Mugs $200
- Shirts $400
- Pens $200

Sommelier $500

Total cost $3,380.50
Cost per ticket $50
Number of expected attendees 150
Break-event line (total cost divided by expected number) 70

In this example, you will need to have at least seventy attendees to break even. The devil is in the details, however. For example, can you get a wine permit? Is there a trusted wine steward in your area that would lend credibility to the event? Is a wine tasting likely to offend (think here of things like church groups or MADD)? You should also try to find out if it has even been done, and if so, how long ago. It goes without saying that if you live in a dry county where such a thing can still be done under certain restrictions.

You will note a line in the example above for invitations. This is an important point that should not be overlooked. In every community, there are power brokers you will want to court in one manner or another. You can do this by sending them special invitations. These are individuals who have influence, wealth, status or all three. Given that the roots of librarianship are firmly in the soil of the idea of the common man, this may seem to some as the height of elitism or even arrogance. While in the best of all possible worlds this would not be necessary—one of America's founders, James Madison, writes that if men were angels we wouldn't need government—in this horribly flawed world you cannot do without them.

CONCLUSION

You are now ready to okay your first event. Is it a lot of work? Yes. Will it double what you are required to do? Absolutely. Will library staff be required to take on more work without additional pay? Unquestionably. In many ways, the end does justify the means. In the end, however, you will have made your library a better place by making more services available. And that, in the final analysis is what friends groups are all about.

AT A GLANCE

- Every friends group must eventually have some event, some rallying point, to remind the community of its presence.
- The purpose of the event, along with pointing out the group, can be to raise funds, raise awareness, or to promote general support.

> - The kind of event—annual, semi-annual, or even more frequent—is of less importance than the event itself.
> - The event should, however, conform to the group's mission statement.
> - When planning this event, think BIG.
> - Deciding on the event is step one. There are four parts to making the decision: know your community; know your stakeholders; know how much money you have to spend to make the event successful; and know the history of where you are.
> - Timing of the event, step two, is critical.
> - Locale of the event, step three, can determine turnout.
> - Theme, step four, can provide your community with an easy reminder of who and what your group is about. It also can make the event more festive.
> - Publicity, step five, makes or breaks these events, regardless of purpose.
> - Researching the event, step six, helps to make the event successful in every detail.
> - Budgeting your event, step seven, can help you measure your success.

ENDNOTES

1. R.B. McMillian, "Fundraising on LI Requires Lots of Diligence, Creativity," *Long Island Business News* 48, no. 30 (July 27, 2001): 28.
2. In order not to be associated with views I do not wish to be (I have enough, believe me) I add this qualifying note. No, I am not a rabid vegetarian al la the PETA.
3. C. Wigen, "Food, Friends and Fun" *ALKI: The Washington Library Association Journal* 17, no. 3 (December 2001): 11.
4. "Adventures in Wonderland," *Fund Raising Management* 24, no. 10 (December 1993): 36.
5. See "The Friends of the Medford Public Library" Web page.
6. The "you" here and throughout this book is understood to mean the friends president, executive officer or whomever is running the friends program.
7. Unfortunately, I cannot write, "or friends executive director," or "the friends president." Although the best case is to write this, the actual experience may be that you simply cannot find anyone to take this on. If this is the case, you either do not do it, or play the cards you're dealt.
8. K. Grayson, "We Don't Talk the Talk," *University Business* 5, no. 10 (December 2002): 3.
9. Ibid.

9 SCRUTINIZING YOUR MARKET

If librarians and also friends groups are slow to publicize their enterprises (toot their own horns), they are even less inclined to do feasibility studies.[1] Many librarians might think feasibility studies are good only for major projects, and there is an element of truth in this. But feasibility studies also provide another important service, and that is to tell whoever wants to know where the library's projects are in a given community's thinking. A feasibility study should be seen as revealing the place where the library must begin making its case. Beginning any sort of fundraising without a feasibility study is like starting a road trip with the idea that all roads really do lead to Rome. You need to be sure which particular road you need to take to ensure fundraising success. It can lead to folly, or worse, confusion. For example, if a library has been in the community for years, the general assumption may be that "everyone knows about us," and so the effort to raise funds will begin with unproven certainty. It may well be that the "everyone" really amounts to only a few people, or that the given need is either unknown or altogether underappreciated.

> A feasibility study should be seen as revealing the place where the library must begin making its case. Beginning any sort of fundraising without a feasibility study is like starting a road trip with the idea that all roads really do lead to Rome. You need to be sure which particular road you need to take to ensure fundraising success.

When I say any group can use a feasibility study, I mean any but the smallest of enterprises. Feasibility studies are needed even before undertaking a friends group, as far as I am concerned; and here is why. Of course one can assume that everyone will jump on the library bandwagon, and hope for the best. But being in favor of libraries, and contributing to their welfare are two distinctly different matters. A feasibility study will tell you whether the first equals the second.

MAKING THE ASSUMPTIONS UNASSUMING

I will never forget the first friends group with which I was involved. The college had been part—a very significant part—of a small community for more than one hundred years. Indeed, as a church-related institution, the college and the largest church in the area shared the same founder and were family-name mainstays of the community. Naturally enough, I assumed that most were aware of the library, a

119

small facility with many of its namesake still in the areas and connected to the college. Moreover, the grand dame of the library, in her late eighties at the time, was still very much an active part of the community, the church, and the library. She came to the library weekly, and she sat in the same pew at the church that her namesake had founded. Her extended family maintained one of the larger companies in the area. Imagine my surprise, when I began making talks around town about the library, only to discover that no one really knew much about it. They did not really understand why we needed any money or grasp beyond a "mere" understanding why I should bother trying to raise funds in addition to the annual budget anyway. Were not the annual funds—surely all we would ever need—automatically part of the general fund-raising anyway?

Part of the reason for this ignorance had to do with what has already been covered in earlier chapters. Some non-library folks simply did not understand what costly ventures libraries are (the proverbial financial black holes). Prior library administrations did not make the case and, if truth be told, did not need to make the case since library expenses had not risen much during those preceding years. Whether great luck, or devilish misfortune, I came to the library at the same time that the cost to acquire library resources had tripled, and the college itself had fallen on hard times, nearly to the point of collapse. The college had secured its survival, but required much library rebuilding, including some significant catch-up purchasing during the very lean years prior to the college's take over by those with stronger financial resources. A feasibility study would have revealed this general ignorance right away, but I did not know about such tools and, at the time, none were considered a standard part of most library fund-raising ventures.

FEASIBILITY STUDIES TODAY

Today's climate is significantly different *vis-à-vis* feasibility studies. Many fund-raising ventures include some sort of feasibility study. Unfortunately, libraries still lag behind in this important part of fund-raising, so this chapter dwells upon their importance, how they should be conducted, and why friends groups need to consider them.

The evidence of slow embrace of these studies is revealed in the paucity of materials returned from both an online and conventional paper index searches. Indeed, in order to find anything about feasibility studies it was necessary to broaden the search to include articles about fund-raising in general. Does this mean that such studies are unnecessary for libraries? Some think so. On the other hand, it is more likely that major library projects were folded into general fund-raising ventures that were undertaken by non-library fund-raisers. Is there danger in this approach? Is it not more reasonable to leave such "arcane" matters, at least as far as friends groups are concerned, to the fund-raising experts?

REASONS FOR MAKING IT FEASIBLE

If there is no other way to get the library on the fund-raising radar screen, then of course being part of a larger effort is better than not being a part at all. In the best of all possible worlds, however, not placing the library in a feasibility study only because it has not been a very prominent part of fund-raising is no excuse, and a poor reason in any case. Feasibility studies provide excellent data that any library can put to good use for nearly any reason. There are at least five reasons why you should insist on undertaking a feasibility at some point in your friends organization. Feasibility studies tell you

1. about your market;
2. about the extent (or reach) of that market;
3. what that market will bear in terms of minimum and maximum dollars for whatever you're trying to accomplish;
4. the potential projects you should undertake; and
5. which ones you should undertake first.

> **Feasibility studies tell you:**
>
> - about your market;
> - about the extent (or reach) of that market;
> - what that market will bear in terms of minimum and maximum dollars for whatever you're trying to accomplish;
> - the potential projects you should undertake; and
> - which ones you should undertake first.

A FEASIBLE OBJECTION

Before delving in to each of these, a potential objection should be addressed. Are not all of these things covered by the organization's general fund-raising outreaches anyway? That is, won't any good fund-raising arm (regardless of its kind) take all of this into consideration for the library? Yes and no. If, for example, you work in a public library, the feasibility study may have been done by your chamber for nonprofit groups in general, and may or may not have anything to tell you about a given library project. If you work in a special library, your feasibility study make have included area museums or the outreach activities of other private nonprofits. While this information is not useless by any means, it does not address specifically what you need to know about library constituents.

Finally, if you work in a college or university library, the last feasibility study may have included a number of projects, including some athletic facilities. Again, the overall picture is doubtless too broad for your purposes. This is not to imply that those who give to athletic facilities or projects will not also give to libraries. (Indeed, coaches like Joe Paterno and the ever-pugnacious Bobby Knight have shown themselves indispensable to library fund-raising.) The point is that you will have a very general picture of projects associated with your institution rather than with the library per se. In many cases, I suspect that the actual interest may be much higher than the general picture, especially if you are able to connect the dots between how funds for the library aid and abet every career, as opposed to funding that addresses the needs of only one career.

So, given the five categories above, how does a feasibility study help you?[2]

Your market. Be honest. Have you ever really given any thought to the library's "market" in the first place? For most of us who toil in the groves of academe, we take our markets seriously in terms of service but hardly anything else. For many, fund-raising of any kind, including friends groups, is not really linked to anything we do other than "general support." In order to turn that support into serious fund-raising potential, including friends groups, you need to know the general characteristics of that group. First of all, you need to know who makes up that group and why they use your library in particular, and would want to be a part of your friends group. You also need to know some demographic information about them. Are they clustered in any one place in particular? What are some of their characteristics? Do they use the library regularly? For what reasons? What is the median age? Are they capable of giving and if so, how much? These and many other kinds of information will be forthcoming from a well-done library feasibility study.

In the case of academic friends groups, the natural and common sense assumption is that most of the friends will have some connection with the college or university. But if you stop there, you will never get beyond it. Every college or university in every city or hamlet provides substantial economic potential for that community. The library, too, provides substantial services that, if not present, would mean a colossal loss of resource potential. A specific study focusing on the library will tell you just how much.

Again, a feasibility study of your general market will tell you almost nothing and may in fact be unnecessary or even useless.[3] It will do you little if any good to have a study that tells you more about potential non-library donors than those who are already open to your story. You need to find those individuals in your market who do not have to "learn" about you or your operation before they can begin to think about

> A well-done library feasibility study will give you the "breadth, depth, and width," of your library market.

a gift. A well-done library feasibility study will give you the "breadth, depth, and width," of your library market. Although most such studies are done for major capital campaigns, I do not want to understate the usefulness of such studies even if your capital campaign is many weeks or months away, or is not even for a capital campaign.

A good study can also prevent major failures of such campaigns even before they begin. How often have you heard about campaigns—not just library ones—that suddenly trim the overall goal or shut down altogether? While the general economy has a great deal to do with this, other things impede overall fund-raising efforts. Take America's recent history, for example. After 9/11, any fund-raising unconnected to the tragedy had little hope of success. This was as it should be, of course, but even a year later, many charitable groups found the financial sledding very tough going if they had little or nothing to do with 9/11. Meanwhile 9/11 fund-raising has been oversubscribed. Even without a national tragedy of the scope of 9/11, many fund-raising ventures fail because of nothing other than poor planning, a looking for fish in dry-bed streams.

The Extent of Your Market. While raising funds for libraries is rather simple once you get the hang of it, getting there is not an easy road. Just how large (or small) is your market? Does it extend beyond your community, your county, your region, or your state? Dacus library is located in the medium-size South Carolina town of Rock Hill. We are twenty-five minutes from Charlotte, North Carolina, and all air traffic is judged from that vantage point. Greenville, South Carolina has an excellent airport facility but it is more than ninety minutes away. Even though the Greenville airfares are much, much cheaper, many guests would much rather pay the extra fare and arrive so much closer. (And if truth be told, many of us who return them to the airport at 7 a.m. much prefer the shorter distance than a two-hour travel-time at that hour.)

What does all of this mean? That a feasibility study tells us whether our reach extends beyond our immediate locale and to what other regions. An academic institution will of course look everywhere there are alumni, but there are other footholds that need to be known. This is not as "intuitive" as you might suspect, if there are many competitors in a small region. A feasibility study would tell you where your market can legitimately begin and end, as well as what sort of probable success you will have in an area where your graduates might not be as plentiful as you would like.

A feasibility study will tell you the "reach" of your market and how you might fare in areas where you have not been, or where you thought might well be controlled by others. At any rate, unless you do a study, you are not likely to know beyond mere guesswork, and that can be as good (and as bad) as the person doing the guessing. Such a study will also give you "ammunition" to take on areas that might have been thought off limits. Because non-library individuals have such odd notions about libraries in the first place, the absence of a feasibility study will doubtless cut you off from areas of fund-raising with significant potential.

What Your Market Will Bear. If feasibility studies do anything well, they provide you with reliable data about the fund-raising potential in your area. Earlier I wrote about giving a friends talk in the coalfields of Virginia. Given the relative poverty of those areas in general, one might think that the largest gift would be mere hundreds. But studies in these areas have shown it to be four or five times higher than this, given the project and the success of making the case there. I suspect the same is true for many areas.

One cannot know where to begin, much less end, without prospect data and the ability of the market to bear various categories of giving. Without a feasibility study, you cannot know if the "big" gift you expect of five thousand dollars should really be fifty thousand dollars. How can you know without anything better than "hunch" data to go on? Like books where covers tell you little, how a person looks or acts tells you very little about their giving potential. A colleague tells the story about one individual who appeared to be able to give a ten thousand dollar gift, and plans were made to make this case. A little extra work, however, revealed that this particular individual had made a gift of over one million dollars to another nonprofit organization a few years before. Imagine the horror of discovering this after the fact.

But finding out about what your market will bear deals with more than just dollars. It has everything to do with the type of fund-raising project and whether or not it has any validity in the area where you expect to conduct it. Failing to find this out ahead of time may force you into very unflattering, face-saving mechanisms, such as having to "suspend" the venture, having to reduce the overall amount sought, or, worse of all, having to cancel it outright.

Potential Successful Projects. A well-done feasibility study will also tell you what your potential is for various kinds of projects. For example, a study might tell you that the market will bear (at the time of the study) a project for an addition, but not for a new building. Or it may reveal that an endowment fund for your monographs budget is the right project to undertake right now. What it cannot do, however, is tell you what to fish for. Rather, it reveals to you whether the specific fish you are requesting swim in the given pond in which you are choosing to fish. In other words, feasibility studies are not "fishing expeditions," so much as they are expeditions for variously proposed species. The structure of the study has to be such that you ask a given question about a particular project, not "Can I raise $500,000?" You may or you may not, depending on the purpose you specify.

> If feasibility studies do anything well, they provide you with reliable data about the fund-raising potential in your area.

FEASIBILITY: STUDYING AND LEARNING

Likewise, a feasibility study can predict failures. Take, for example, the Dulles Greenway project in Virginia. Although not library-related at all, the project has much to teach. This highly touted $340 million privately financed toll road began laying off workers and fretting over making even one loan repayment not three months after its completion.[4] Greenway began the project by ignoring feasibility studies and the changing conditions reflected in them. Those studies revealed that while early toll roads had been highly successful, the most recent ones were failing, and very badly. Collections were down as much as fifty percent in some cases. Furthermore, though the economic predictions were very poor to murky, the torpedoes were damned and full throttle was thrust. Cohen makes the very important point that the feasibility studies not only have to be done and have a limited shelf-life, they also have to be listened to.

This story illustrates what I have argued throughout this chapter, namely that feasibility studies are more or less "market research."[5] If you were running a business rather than a library, you would never introduce a new product to the market without first testing it. In the same manner, you should never undertake a fund-raising venture without first seeing if it can be done, and if it can be done where you intend to do it.

Feasibility studies also save face. When the executive director of Camp Ronald McDonald for Good Times wanted to build a multi-million dollar facility, she never hesitated about the study. Having the right hunch about the right number of dollars had to be verified somehow and she felt the feasibility study would do that.[6] If, for example, you plan a project that will cost twice the amount your study says you can raise, then perhaps doing two campaigns would be better. Getting the full amount over time is much better that trying to get it all at once and failing.

When to Undertake Your Project. Lastly, feasibility studies will provide some background on when you should try to raise you funds. The feasibility study does not turn ordinary people into crystal ball gazers. Rather it lets you, like a physician, take the pulse, so to say, of the community, and decide if the patient is well or ill. If you get back data that indicates your community is harder hit by economic downturns than the nation in general, it may be best to alter the timing of your campaign. On the other hand, it may tell you that now is a good time, but a few months later may be even better.

A study will give you the data necessary to make an informed decision. Of course nothing is infallible. Indeed, some argue that feasibility studies are unnecessary, because they do not reveal anything new for

> Feasability studies help you figure out when to undertake your fundraising project.

too high a price.[7] If funds are tight, why bother with useless studies? If the funding study is done well it is highly unlikely it will reveal nothing new. But that is the key. Finding the right group to conduct your study means everything. This requires investigating not only the company, but also its clients. Feasibility studies fail when they are not conducted by the right personnel, or when they match the right company with the wrong project.[8] For example, the company may not have done a library feasibility study. Or perhaps it has done some but only a handful under very limited circumstances with marginal results. The key is to study before choosing.

Some studies match the wrong parties. Perhaps the board wants one, but library personnel do not. Or perhaps the study is done to "prove" what is already hoped for, or worse, assumed to be true. Such results can only spell disaster. Libraries should look to those who have done numerous library studies, and then should be willing to abide by the findings.

As far as the cost objection goes—feasibility studies are expensive—it is largely true. Feasibility studies can cost upwards of ten thousand dollars. If money is tight anyway, some may feel that the feasibility study adds nothing, while taking too much away. Suppose, for example, you are thinking of adding an additional floor to your library for a cost of $2 million. The feasibility study costs twenty-five thousand dollars. Isn't the argument sound that you could equip a room for that kind of money?

Yes and no. Sure, twenty-five thousand dollars—or whatever the cost turns out to be—is not cheap. On the other hand the study could save you twice that, or even more. If done well, it could more than pay for itself by providing you with important information about your community that you can turn into more explicit dollars. Apart from these things, it also makes good business sense as you would never undertake a library service for which there was no audience. The fact that you have one for a given service is your feasibility study in a nutshell.

The other legitimate argument is that feasibility studies are time consuming. The simple fact of the matter is, they are. Much of the time spent in the study preparation has to do with the study's subject, in this case, the library. Do you have a good strategic vision? It is important that you know what your vision is, but much more important that your staff knows it, and can articulate it in some way. Further, do you have good vision and mission statements, do you have both short and long-term goals, and have you operationalized these goals into achievable objectives? Most institutions that complain about the time factor in feasibility studies may be telling more about themselves than they wish others to know. It all comes down to homework and whether you have been doing it over the years. If you have, you most likely can cut the time of the study in half. If not, you will be in for a long haul. What is more, staff will eventually complain that "all this feasibility study is doing is giving me more work!"

Along the way the study may turn up something about the library that you did not know, or did but ignored. For example, personnel issues in libraries tend to abound. Whether it is our predilection for the eccentric or merely the nature of library work itself doesn't matter. The fact is that library personnel can be a difficult lot. Suppose, however, that a rather major issue reveals itself in the form of mostly negative expressions on the part of the staff, or your clientele about your staff. You have to fix those things or forget going forward for they will come out during the fund-raising element later.[9]

Successful feasibility studies provide a great deal of confidence for your library because it proves that your goals are actually possible to attain. Without one you really have not much to go on. What happens when the first few gifts prove a devil of a time to get? Will people get discouraged? Will staff begin acting out self-fulfilling prophecies? Will the larger administration of your library pull the plug on the friends project? Without the study you have nothing to point to for confidence in what your group is trying to do other than the fact that you are doing it and you think it can be done. You cannot point to some third party evaluation that will provide the calming salve to keep going when things look pretty dismal. With a study in hand when the going gets tough you can use the report to instill confidence, rebuild confidence that has been broken down, or stiffen the resolve of those who are easily cowed.

Can you conduct your own feasibility study without third party interference? That is doubtful. Not only would it take the average library staff months to come to grips with what is needed and why, it would also take personnel away from their daily tasks. Moreover, you would lose one of the very important and key ingredients of the study: third party evaluation and perspective. Doing your own feasibility study is not much different from filling out your own "summary" evaluation. There is little chance that you will receive much negative feedback in the report. What you want is a calculating, cold eye examination of what can be done and whether you have the right stuff to do it.

Can you conduct one without the support of your friends and larger administration? Not likely. Your larger board or administration has to be with you on this, as with all important things. Without that support, you may not be able to complete the study, or even get it off the ground. Moreover, you may encounter some resistance to spending the money (see costs, above) in the first place, if you have not done the hard work of bringing everyone on board.

WHO DOES FEASIBILITY STUDIES

The best, and really the only, library feasibility studies group I know of is Library Funding Associates. Bill Mott, its president, has been doing them for years and has a record of success (and clients) to prove it. In the interest of full disclosure, I must add that Bill is a personal friend. He and I were in library school together and have kept up since that time, now twenty years later. I can say that while Bill has done a few seminars for me, he has never done a feasibility study for me. But if you need one, Library Funding Associates may be the place to begin. Surf over to www.libraryfunding.com and decide for yourself.

CONCLUSION

Feasibility studies provide much-needed information for making your case for raising significant gifts. The study can return important data that you can use for a given task, or use later for entirely different purposes. Although complex and expensive, it is unlikely that members of your friends group will either be familiar with the studies, or know those who are. It cannot hurt your library to use feasibility studies for your fund-raising efforts. On the contrary, it can augment those efforts in such a way to make the entire fund-raising experience a win-win proposition.

AT A GLANCE

- Feasibility studies can be your group's best friend.
- Unfortunately, libraries, and Friends Groups, often ignore them at their peril.
- The study should be tailored as closely as possible to what the Friends Group is hoping to accomplish whether its for some building plan, or simply to increase membership.
- Feasibility studies will help you learn as much as you can about your particular market.
- Not only will you learn what that market it, but its extent, what it will bear, but also the potential for various kinds of projects.
- Such studies often will help you understand when to undertake a given kind of project.

> - There is no free lunch and feasibility studies are costly. But if done well, you will reap their benefits for years to come.
> - Bill Mott of Library Associates runs a company devoted to doing library feasibility studies.

ENDNOTES

1. The best firm, and perhaps the only one in the library field, is Library Associates, Inc. My good friend Bill Mott is the president and his work in this area is unequaled. See www.libraryassociates.com.

2. While I believe that feasibility studies can be done for any project whether connected to funds or not, the rest of the chapter will consider feasibility studies from their more common venue of fund-raising.

3. See the pros and cons of feasibility studies in B.J. Harrison, "Feasibility Study ... Can we Scale this Height?" *Fund Raising Management* 27, no. 3 (May 1996): 16–20.

4. N. Cohen, "White Elephants: Why Some Large Projects Fail," *Government Finance Review* 12, no. 2 (April 1996): 28–31.

5. Harrison, 16.

6. Harrison, 17.

7. See, for example, T.K. Goodale, "Is it feasible?" *Fund Raising Management* 32, no. 9 (November 2001): 40–42. Even Goodale believes the benefits fare outweigh the defects.

8. Harrison, 18.

9. Harrison makes this point and others in non-library contexts but they are instructive nevertheless.

10 PERPETUATING FRIENDS

> It is the friends coordinator's task to perpetuate the group.

Your group is up, it is running, and you are successful. Now you can sit back and relax, right? Not really. One of the least appreciated tasks of the friends coordinator is this last one: perpetuating the group. Let me preface my comments with two introductory comments.

First, if all your group ever aspires to accomplish is to raise funds of no more than four figures, or buy a few books, maybe one computer every now and again, you can ignore this chapter. No one can demand that all friends groups must aspire to what I have written here, though I believe the most successful will pattern themselves in a manner like this. If you would like to have the possibility of taking on larger, more vital projects, however, then designing the group to do more is required from the beginning, and so here is this chapter. Second, in order to achieve this you, as coordinator, must undertake the tasks below. If you do all this as an unpaid volunteer, so much the better. If not, it is likely that the director and the friends president will have to work together. This chapter is written from the point-of-view of the second, and more likely, scenario.[1]

As we have seen, it is hard work establishing a group where no group has existed. It is harder still to establish an effective group to do what is necessary. And it is no simple task, either, coordinating all the activities of the friends. All of these things take time, devotion and, above all, commitment. It would be nice if we lived in some Periclean Age in which one hundred percent of both budgets and needs were met by the annual funding received. That happens only in Camelot, if anywhere.

THANKLESS TASK # 3,408

Nevertheless, we identify any one task as the most thankless, it may well be this one: perpetuating your group from year to year and maintaining both its fund-raising enthusiasm and its effective operation. Unfortunately there is nothing Cartesian about the world of friends groups: no one can set it into motion and simply sit back and let it tick. It requires nurturing and the kind of nurturing such as one would apply

> **TIP:** Think of gardening when planning to perpetuate effective friends groups from year to year: Plant, irrigate, weed, cultivate, prune and harvest.

to a garden. And like the garden, if you cultivate well, you reap a bountiful harvest.

Not to put too fine a point on it, with the garden metaphor in mind, what is it that has to be done to perpetuate effective friends groups from year to year? It falls under several categories: Planting, irrigation, weeding, cultivating, pruning and harvesting. I don't mean to sound overly agrarian, or stultifyingly pedestrian. Rather, because the analogy works so well, it provides a helpful rubric for knowing what to do, and when to do it. Bear with me and I think you will see exactly what I mean.

PLANTING THE RIGHT SEEDS

Successful friends groups have an active coordinator who is routinely recruiting new members. This person may be scheduling lunches, calling on businesses and business people, or "simply" making the rounds of the civic clubs and activities to see and be seen. Both are important, but the latter may be more important and perhaps least acted upon. Your community needs to know who you are and why you are present at various functions, and why your group needs them. In the same way that politicians like to be seen with important constituents, and associated with various and sundry worthy projects, you, too, as "operations manager" of the friends need to be seen by many, and for the same reasons. It may be helpful to think of this as planting the right seeds. This must begin from day one, and continue with each friends coordinator.

> Successful friends groups have an active coordinator who is routinely recruiting new members.

SEE AND BE SEEN

It is not enough that those in your community see the library. They have to associate it with your friends group. That is going to be hard to do if the person representing the friends group is not "visible" in the community. This most easily is the dean or director, as I have said before; but again, it does not have to be if an unpaid coordinator can be found who will undertake the same role.

As an example of how this works, take a look at the United Way campaign. For about four months, the paper, the radio, and businesses are bombarded with the "visibility" of that campaign. Nearly every place you go you see the familiar "money thermometer" with it's bulging red bulb showing how close (or far away) the community is from reaching its preestablished goal. In many ways, you cannot get away from the campaign when it is in full swing. (Only lately have unseemly practices at the national level—and below—darkened what was otherwise a "whistle-clean" operation. This, too, is another good lesson to learn.)

Of course a friends groups may not be able to gain this kind of prominence but there is no law or rule that says you cannot try. Besides, certain programs do achieve this status, such as pointed out in Chapter 1, and the fact that they mimic other national campaigns is neither luck of the draw nor unusual coincidence. The point is that you got to establish a "presence" in the community so that when folks see the coordinator they think "friends group." This can be done a number of ways.

BECOME A PRESENCE IN YOUR COMMUNITY

> **TIP:** Become a presence in your community. Plan events such as "fun runs," "the mother of all book sales," and innovative community dinners that will establish your group in the community.

For example, I mentioned earlier the annual friends dinners hosted by the library where I once worked. These became so popular with the community that eventually I could go almost anywhere and folks would stop me and ask, "Who's coming this year?" That is exactly the kind of response you're looking for.

There are other ways of achieving this than a dinner, of course. For example, it can be an annual "fun run," or the "mother of all book sales," or something else.[2] The event (see Chapter 8 on events) merely establishes your group; it is up to you, the friends coordinator, to "connect the dots" between the library and group so that the right associations will be established.

For example, this person can try to get on every possible speaking venue, as well as on the local paper's editorial page. The idea is to link the coordinator with the library and the group as quickly as possible. Since civic groups are always needing speakers, and local papers enjoy editorials written by local folks, strike quickly and often.

This, or something very like it, does several things. First, it establishes the coordinator as spokesperson for the group and alerts all future storywriters that you are the source for friends news. Second, it brings your program to the foreground so that people will begin thinking, perhaps for the very first time, about the library represented by the group and how the needs of that library are not solved by annual budgets. Third, it exposes to a rather large audience, both in person and in writing, that your group (and therefore the library) is in a leadership position and they need to take notice. Eventually, you will have people calling you, rather than you calling them. Follow this process, or something very like it, and you are certain to succeed in getting the people required to sustain the group.

IRRIGATING YOUR HARVEST

To make a garden flourish you need water, and to make your friends group grow you must provide them with regular communication, the "water" of a thriving group. Chapter 2 touched on this in detail so it will not be necessary to repeat it here. Rather, it may be helpful to point out that the kinds of communication you need are both corporate and personal. You will make contact with members at regular events, at board meetings, at various other functions your group hosts, or your group cohosts with others. Do not forget the other important times at which you can also make contact. You will see them as you go about your personal business and it is always important to make sure you do not miss out on opportunities to speak with them. It is especially important that you do not seek "to do business" so much as you are trying to build a relationship. Loyal memberships come through relationships and little else. Other personal contacts will of course occur. The circumspect friends leader will be ready to make those contacts and assure his program of continued success. What are some other ways?

Remembering birthdays or other special occasions are always a plus. Obviously even with a very small membership one could not keep up with all the birthdays of every group member, but with Palm technology, one can keep up with a considerable number.[3] Of course, how you keep up with it isn't important; what is important is that you make the effort to "make contact." A card here and there does wonders. And what does it cost you beyond a few minutes and a postage stamp?

> To make your friends group grow you must provide them with regular communication, the "watering" of a thriving group.

FRIENDS E-DEEDS

The same is true with e-mails. Sending out notices or other "reminders" of one kind or another is a great way to keep "irrigating" your membership. The idea is to have your name as coordinator never far from their lips. Most friends coordinators allow too much time to pass between one event and another. But this misses important opportunities. These points of contact need not be elaborate or "information-packed." They are not substitutes for the newsletter or any other type of formal communication. Rather these are simple ways to keep some communication going all year, and keep your group alive to those it should most matter.

By now it should be obvious that almost anything the friends coordinator does will help keep the lines of communication open. It is little more than good common sense when you think about it. How does any relationship survive, whether it is through friendship, blood, or marriage? By keeping the lines of communication open and active, that is how.

LILIES THAT FESTER

If you have ever had a summer garden you know, unless your area has been drought-stricken, that weeds are not only a common enemy, but also will choke your garden to death if left unattended. Living in the South as I do, I get to watch the kudzu overtake a wooded lot adjacent to our home. It amazes me every year. In winter, it dies away with positively no trace. With the arrival of spring, there it is, and one week later it has covered even the tallest of trees.

Of course nothing like that happens within friends groups, but something similar does. Membership stagnates while dollars go nowhere. What do you do? The easiest course of action is to ignore it, and seven out of ten friends groups coordinators do. But this is not the best course of action, especially if the member is also a board member or someone in a leadership role. If you have made your case plainly and told everyone what is expected of them when they sign on in a leadership capacity, then you owe it to the group, and to the other leaders on your board, to take action.

Many times it is nothing more than that a certain person felt he or she was being ignored. A call, a letter or a lunch, can straighten out everything and soon you will see this person back on track. Occasionally, for whatever reason, a person will come to your group who will do positively nothing. He or she may attend events, but nothing more. If you want to see your group thrive, a personal visit will help you enormously.

Other members may go in the other direction. These you do not have to "weed" so much as you have to curtail their activities. For example, you may be lucky enough to have very active members who begin the group's fund-rasing activities without you. He or she may undertake to call on individuals with or—more likely the case—without prior notification. This can cause some difficulties and even possible embarrassment if you do not act, and quickly. You may have waited for a good reason. A campaign for another project (or altogether different entity that would conflict with your own) may be winding down and you want the "down" time to allow for separation between the projects.

Saying nothing to your over-zealous member will only result in greater damage later. Telling your volunteer why it is important to wait should be all that is required. A good member will understand and bridle his enthusiasm until it can be put to better use. Again, communication is the key.

CULTIVATION

Some potential friends may have to be "wooed," while others with substantial finances may have to be coaxed and cajoled. In some cases you may need to consult professional help—development officers or other similar personnel—to provide you with the necessary background to make the right pitch. Facing major donors can be a daunting experience and oftentimes saying the right thing at the right time makes all the difference in the world. It is not that librarians cannot or are not capable of doing this; it is more that we do not have much training in this area (see Chapter 1) and need to consult the experts.[4] Again, if all that is desired out of the friends group is several hundred fifty-dollar members, then do nothing. But if the group wants more (and the library needs it) the group will have to go after larger contributors. Again, building a relationship is the only way.

Cultivation takes on many forms. It can take a year or more, and in some cases, depending on the size of the gift, even longer. Those who are fortunate enough to have considerable largess to bestow are not quick to fritter it away. (Perhaps one of the synonyms of "wealthy" may be "prudent.") It takes time to ask for tens of thousands of dollars, as well it should. How many of us much less wealthy take months to buy a car? Why should it be any different with those who have that amount to give away?

These individuals want to know that what they are giving to is worthy of their largess. Part of the cultivation will be spent in proving the group's worth. What do you do? Why it is important? How does it help the community (this is extremely important since most already know it will help your group)? These are but a very few of the many questions you will have to answer as you spend time cultivating members.

Second, they want to know that you are capable of bringing off whatever it is you say the group can do.[5] They need to know how your organization is structured, who runs it, what the budget is and how it is dispensed. They will also want to know a great deal about the library the group represents. You cannot go into these meetings unprepared and expect to be successful. You must be willing to divulge as much information as is necessary to prove this. Moreover, you certainly do not want to present a budget that you have not yourself gone over with painstaking care.

What all this comes down to is that you are always doing things throughout the friends partnership that make it possible for you to maintain the friends you make as you acquire new ones. This is what staying power in friends groups is all about.

HARVESTING

Perhaps the easiest part of perpetuating your group, but the most despised by nearly every friends coordinator, is the harvesting. This is that part of the work where you bring people together and "close the deal," as it were. If you wait for them to come forward, you may be waiting a very long time. If you never ask, you may miss out on grand opportunities. How does this perpetuate your group? It makes goals attainable and so attracts others to a successful program. Some may think that because there are five hundred dollar and one thousand dollar memberships, that is all they have to do: let people know this level of giving is possible. But if no effort is made to secure such memberships, it is highly unlikely many will come forward without asking, and without first building a relationship.

How to ask, and what to ask for is neither easy nor intuitive. It requires months of research, research that has been gathered by the friends organization, has been studied, assimilated, and is now acted upon. Timing is everything. If you ask too soon, you may get the answer you do not want while spoiling any chances of getting anything later. If you wait too long, commitment may get made to others that will preclude any chance you have of getting one for your group.

Will you make mistakes? Of course. They are inevitable. Because raising funds of any kind are predicated on the caprice of human nature—yours and your donors—there is little chance that you can, over the long haul, avoid mistakes. But you learn from them and are better prepared for the next time. Not only will you make mistakes of asking both too early and too late, you will also ask for the wrong amount. But in the latter case, research helps. It is always better to ask for too much than too little. People are never offended by being thought too well off than they are being thought otherwise.

Some reading these words will no doubt be puzzled. They will wonder why any asking needs to be done at all. Are not all friends groups made up of those who give twenty five dollars here and one hundred dollars there? Yes and no. All groups have these categories. They also have larger portions of their memberships giving these amounts than they do those who give ten times those amounts. But few groups survive for many years without larger gifts being made. Some groups are fortunate to have donors who give larger amounts automatically. Public libraries in cities like Los Angeles and Dallas have their donors who contribute many thousands every year. (These are not automatic in the sense that they have not been cultivated.) For most libraries, however donors must be discovered, cultivated and finally harvested for the cause. Without them, whether they number only one or two, or one or two dozen, friends groups at those libraries will never amount to more than nominal support and require yet another form of fund-raising to accomplish stated goals.

All of these thing—planting, irrigation, cultivation and harvesting—are important parts of perpetuating your friends group. It helps if you establish a plan early and follow it through to its end. But what about those groups that are already in place and have been for years? What do they say is important?

GROUPS WITH LONGEVITY

Those are the theoretical musings that have been gleaned from research, but what about the experience of long-lasting groups? Three groups that have had startlingly healthy staying power were asked to "come clean" about what made their groups work. Here is what they said.

FRIENDS OF THE WELLES-TURNER LIBRARY

Lillian Levin of the Friends of the Welles-Turner Library in Glastonbury, Connecticut wrote to tell me the group is now entering its thirty-first year. Formed in 1972, Ms. Levin has been involved with the group since 1988, serving as a board member, treasurer, membership chair, vice president and president over the years. Glastonbury is a small town, or perhaps more accurately, township of twenty-nine thousand. The membership in the friends group is a whopping one thousand four hundred, or about six percent of the entire population. To what can we attribute this incredible support and remarkable longevity?

Interestingly, and without any prompting on my part, Ms. Levin writes that "Support from the Library Director and staff" as the number one ingredient. The director is an ex officio member and attends the bimonthly meetings. If she cannot attend, she sends her designee. Akin to this support is an equally supportive library board. All library board members are dues-paying members of the friends and there is a liaison from one group to the other. All support the activities of the friends. In 2002, the friends group brought in fifty thousand dollars for items not covered by the annual budget.

Advocacy. Advocacy also ranks high with Ms. Levin. Even during two failed referenda occurring over very poor economic times, the friends support "never wavered." During one referendum for library expansion, over one hundred friends members attended town council meetings and spoke in favor of the expansion. The third time proved the charm.

Community Involvement. Community involvement also ranks very high. The friends group sponsors two eight-hour book sales. Last year they raised almost forty thousand dollars from these two events. Most community members volunteer for service and the proceeds are used by the library. They also use some of the proceeds to provide books for the homebound, and to visit with them when they can. The group also provides museums passes for the public to enter the local museum for free, or for a reduced rate. This combination of helping the library and the community is a sure winner.

Communication. Communication is also paramount with this friends group as they fund the library newsletter. They also provide funding for library staff development for travel to conferences, continuing education and the like.

Funds Multiple Items. Finally, the group funds multiple items for the library, including books but also CDs, DVDs, audio books, computer work stations, cabinets, furniture and software. Every item purchased by the friends has a plaque or an adhesive sticker indicating its point of origination. This, too, is obviously a form of communication and it communicates the best kind of information: this group is here to help everyone in the community.

The Friends of Welles-Turner Memorial Library is doubly lucky in being able to take advantage of the Friends of Connecticut Libraries Association which is itself funded by a grant from the Libraries Services and Construction Act (LSCA). A very handy brochure outlines the duties of the library director, trustee, and friend as each take a role in administrative, policy, planning, marketing, fiscal activities, legislative activities, meetings and networking. It should be pointed out that the friends group is also a part of the Friends of the Library U.S.A.

FRIENDS OF THE HASTINGS, NEBRASKA PUBLIC LIBRARY

Felicia Cogley of the Friends of the Hastings, Nebraska Public Library wrote to explain the longevity of its group. The friends group there began in 1984, aligning itself with the Library Foundation and six library supporters. In 1985 it had grown to fifty-two members and today is over four hundred seventy members and volunteers more than two thousand five hundred hours of library service.

Ms. Cogley knows all about the difficulty in keeping the group alive. At one point in this group twenty-year history the board fell apart, membership dropped and leadership roles became all but impossible to fill. They solved it by hiring a friends coordinator—one person who stood in charge of the activities of the group—that became a permanent position. This coordinator maintain records, plan board agendas, recruit volunteers and, "most importantly, keeps the lines of communication [open]…in an ongoing and consistent manner." Ms. Cogley attributes longevity to the following.

Communication. All of the activities of all the library's support groups, members, staff, volunteers and the like are kept apprised of the other concerns. They attend one another's meetings or report on same in the library's newsletter with a circulation list of one thousand, which goes to all of the above, plus key community leaders.

Organization. The friends group reorganized in 1992 and follows strict terms of office as determined by its bylaws/constitution. Ms. Cogley writes, again without prompting, "Each person knows his position is important and will be missed if absent….Officers who have trouble with attendance are replaced."

Persistence. What works with one community, says Ms Cogley, "may not work with another," so it is important to keep trying until something does. We try, fail, evaluate "and move forward."

Fun. Ms. Cogley points out that the key to keeping the group fresh each year is that they "take the time" to enjoy one another's company "while working our mission to be of help to our library." Again, it doesn't hurt that this group, too, is part of the Friends of the Library U.S.A.

FRIENDS OF THE PICKERING OHIO PUBLIC LIBRARY

Finally, Lisa Reade of the Friends of the Pickering Ohio Public Library had this to say. The group began in 1989. Until Ms. Reade came on board, the group had book sales twice a year but spent little money. Ms. Reade secured the 501(C)3 status and then began increasing the group's visibility. She stressed the following.

Communication. "First and foremost [people who donate money] need to know we exist and why we want their money," she writes. So, she went out and recruited like-minded individuals to raise awareness and money. She also made a trip to see the director of the library and spoke to all staff. "People are tempted to join when they know what the group is about," she stressed.

The Web. "To increase visibility of our friends group we created a Web site which showcases much of our activities. We also participated in an Annual Community Parade with a float for [the library and group]." The group has won awards for its floats and pictures may be seen on the Web site (www.foppl.homestead.com).

Events. In addition to the book sales and the parade, the group also publishes a cookbook, sells candy bars at the Circulation Desk of the library and raffles of beautiful "Literary Baskets" every six to eight weeks. The retail value of these baskets can run as high as two hundred dollars. (See the baskets on the Web.) The book sales are now conducted on Amazon.com and eBay, increasing both awareness, visibility and dollars.

Risks. Ms. Reade is not adverse to risk, either. "Change and innovation is what keeps the group in the spotlight," she writes and with that in mind she bought a fabulous basket in an angel theme just before Easter. The basket was raffled and thus began the Literary Theme baskets mentioned above. At the end of its second year this outreach alone has raised over two thousand five hundred dollars.

Cultivation, Recruitment. Ms. Reade keeps her group self-renewing by believing in just the opposite. "I think [the idea of self-renewing] is the kiss of death," she told me. No volunteer group can be self-renewing unless it is "constantly figur[ing] out ways to recruit new ideas along with people to keep the group fresh."

CONCLUSION

There you have it. The theoretical and the practical. I chose to share these two because they are very different approaches with the same key elements: communication, activities, persistence, advocacy and the like. If this does not convince you that the friends group can be one of your library's most valuable asset, most likely nothing else will. All of the ingredients are here in this blueprint.

All that's left for you to do is follow it.

AT A GLANCE

- Perpetuating friends groups is perhaps the hardest task of all.
- If you plan to have a group that strives only for a few thousands each year, then perpetuating it may not be necessary. On the other hand, if you want a vibrant and continuous group from year to year, perpetuating it is a must.

- Like a well-cultivated garden, friends groups must be groomed.
- Finding a friends coordinator who will do the work required to perpetuate your group is the key. This may be a paid or unpaid individual.
- This chapter assumes a very close working relationship between the friends Coordinator and the head of the library to which it is attached.
- The friends coordinator will have to become a presence within the community by becoming an active member in its civic and nonprofit groups.
- Ongoing communication with your group's members and with potential members can be achieved through cards, letters, e-mails and even "power" lunches.
- Some members of your group, even those in leadership positions, may not be as active as you need them to be. They may require more care, and yes, even weeding.
- Friends groups cannot exist long on fifty-dollar gifts every year from the same one hundred members.
- You may need to cultivate the members of your community who can give much larger amounts. These same members will also have to be "harvested"—eventually the friends Coordinator, working with the library's head, will have to ask for a gift.
- When you ask for a gift, always ask for more than you think you can get. Large-gift donors are never insulted when you ask for too much. In fact, some are insulted if you ask for too small a gift, or worse, they give it and either never give again, or give only that amount every year.
- Three long-lived groups that follow these suggestions are presented in this chapter.

ENDNOTES

1. In all of my research, and even in the examples cited below, no unpaid volunteers who undertook this role were found. This of course does not mean they do not exist but that they are more rare.

2. Some may balk at the possible sexism of this remark but really, "person of all book sales" makes little sense.

3. For example, though not all are friends or even library advisory board members, I keep track of about seventy-five using this technology.

4. The phrase *quiquam in sua arte crendendum* speaks directly to this: believe the experts in their own field.

5. In many cases, I believe this is why so many groups opt for the smaller contributor. They can promise results with the fifty dollar gift. It requires more effort to prove they can deliver for the five hundred or five thousand dollar gift.

A FRIENDS GROUP STARTER KIT

A CREATING EFFECTIVE BYLAWS AND A CONSTITUTION

No matter how small your group may be, you need to have a *Constitution and Bylaws* for it. The establishment of these allows you to create the infrastructure and define the purpose of the group, by means of its committees and terms of office. Further, it provides for the ability to add or subtract from the process by means of a vote of the membership. It is important to think through the process carefully. What you decide in this document, while not set in stone, will be set for the immediate future, until such time as you can establish your group and then make arrangements to vote for its change.

Having said that, it is critical to get such a document in place. Having it ready to provide to would-be members demonstrates concretely how serious you are about the group. Moreover, it adds a degree of thoughtfulness to what you're doing. Those who understand such things—the very ones you seek to impress—will immediately grasp that your bylaws are a colophon of your burgeoning group maturity, and they will be attracted by that, as well as your groups serious *raison d'être*.

So what should the bylaw's contain? Herewith are its parts.

Article I establishes the **name** of your group. This can be the customary title, "Friends of the ___ Library," or you can become clever or imaginative and try to capture your group's name in an otherwise descriptive phrase.

Article II establishes your group's **purpose**. This should not be overly long but it should try to galvanize your members. It can rise to the level of inspiration or it can remain merely straightforward. It should never, however, be pedestrian. By all means, there should be some statement to the effect that one of the group's main reasons for existence is to solicit and receive gifts.

Article III deals with **membership**, or what constitutes membership. Novices may think that this statement can be pandemic, universal in its embrace, but nothing could be farther from the truth. Membership should be open only to those who are in agreement with the purpose of the group. That is, your membership statement should say something to the effect that membership is open to "all those who energetically embrace," or are "fully complicit with the group's stated purposes." The reasons for spelling this out are twofold. First, you don't want members who will become merely "membership matter"—that is, possessing weight and occupying space, but little else. Second, you want to establish early on an understand that this is a fund-raising group. In brief, the establishment of such a clause allows you to rescind membership should it become necessary.

The second part of your membership statement is a line about voting. Do all members have voting rights immediately? Do they acquire the right after a few months or a year? Most bylaws indicate voting is immediate upon joining. I would add that it should be so if and only if the group collects a membership fee. Should you approve collective memberships—say for families, for example—then you need to spell out the number of votes permissible for each collective unit. Failure to do so will only cause confusion later when all ten of the Herdmans try to vote.

Article IV spells out the **officers** that serve in your group, while *Article V* delineates their duties. The offices are typically president, vice president, secretary or secretary-treasurer, or both. Obviously the president serves as the overseer, appoints chairpersons of and/or establishes committees, and serves as an ex officio member of every committee save one, usually the nominating committee. The vice president is a president elect, typically, and this should be spelled out, so folks know what they are getting into when they agree to serve in that capacity. The vice president will also serve in the president's absence. Nothing is more inimical to a new friends group than officers who shirk or bypass their duties. The secretary will record minutes of each meeting, as well as keep track of records, alert members of meetings and the like.

If the group creates a separate treasurer's office (a wise thing to do), that person will collect and deposit dues, and report to the president available funds. Since volunteers serve these capacities, the role of treasure needs to be someone who does not mind some initial time-consuming work. Even established groups face having to have the new treasurer go by the bank and sign the check-signing card. New groups will have to create all of this, as well as file for a charitable status (501(c)3) dispensation from the IRS if incorporated. If funds never exceed $25,000, there will still be some forms to fill out, most notably IRS 991, if only a few lines. When funds exceed the $25,000 threshold, much more is required. You don't want someone in this role, who is not familiar with these things, or is not fully reliable.

Some groups (see below) have both corresponding and recording secretaries, the first charged with the responsibility of keeping up with the membership, as well as keeping same informed, the second with keeping up with the minutes.

The next two *Articles* some groups include to spell out the executive committee and the board of directors. The first is made up of all the officers while the second may consist of all the chairpersons. Such a division of labor establishes a democractic process and allows business to go forward when one or the other cannot (or will not) function as planned. This group structure is not a bad idea but it may weigh down unnecessarily a fledgling group. You want your group to be as representative as possible, but it's unlikely, at least in the early going, that both will be mandatory. A new group may be striving hard just to get officers in place.

Article VIII usually spells out **meetings.** One needs to think small about these and not try to have too many. If more are needed, one duty the president can exercise is to call others as needed. Usually one or two a year is plenty. One can also insert here that X-number of members can call a meeting by asking the president to do so. Ten percent of the membership may be enough unless your membership is unusually small, (under one hundred) in which case just to have more than three in attendance, you may want to specify a higher percentage. You may also want to spell out how the meeting of the executive committee is to be publicized—by e-mail, in the newsletter, in the local newspaper, if it can be done for no charge. You should also specify what constitutes a quorum.

Article IX establishes the kinds of **dues** you will require. These can be as few as three or four and as many as eight or ten. Generally you should set dues at a figure high enough to accomplish what you hope to do. For example, if you set $10 as a due, you'll need many of them to be able to make a difference. But having dues at various levels allows you to overcome this drawback. Each level *should* have restrictions. For example, those who can afford to pay $100 should not be able to pay $10, so the latter can be a "student" due or some such designation. Family dues are also appropriate but again, don't undersell what you're trying to accomplish. Collection of dues should be annual or semiannual and some line should be present in this article that addresses what happens when a person does not pay them. For example, you could say, "Failure to pay the dues within one week (ten days, etc.) of the annual collection will result in a withdrawal of membership."

Article X sets how the **funds** are spent and who determines that. For example, you can say that funds will be spent as determined by the president and the executive committee in conjunction with the library director. The inclusion of the director as the determining factor sets an excellent tone for future working relations. This also prevents the purchase of some item or set of books that may not be something the library can use. Should the unmentionable happen, it is not a bad idea to have a line here to explain what happens to the funds in the event the group dissolves.

Lastly, *Article XI* establishes **parliamentary procedure** and this almost always is a line that reads, "*Robert Rules of Order* Revised governs this groups when not in conflict with these bylaws."

Some friends groups will indicate various committees and describe their duties while others may simply indicate types of committees. Most will allow the duties of the president to cover this function. The latter avoids having to come up at once will the committees you will eventually use. Other articles may establish how **amendments** are to be made to the bylaws, while still others will establish the length of service of each of the executive officers, usually no more than two years.

Below are two sample bylaws.

Bylaws for

FRIENDS OF THE HILLSDALE LIBRARY

ARTICLE I. NAME

Section 1. The name of this organization shall be FRIENDS OF THE HILLSDALE LIBRARY (Hillsdale Library identified hereafter as "the Library").

ARTICLE II. PURPOSE

Section 1. The purpose of this organization shall be to maintain an association of persons interested in libraries; to focus public attention on the Library; to stimulate the use of the Library's resources and services; to receive and encourage gifts, endowments, and bequests to the Library; to support and cooperate with the Library in developing library services and facilities for the community; to lend legislative support where needed; and to support the freedom to read as expressed in the American Library Association Bill of Rights.

ARTICLE III. MEMBERSHIP

Section 1. Membership in this organization shall be open to all individuals in sympathy with its purposes.

Section 2. Each membership shall be entitled to one vote. Each family membership shall be entitled to two votes.

ARTICLE IV. OFFICERS

Section 1. The officers of this organization shall be a president, vice president, treasurer, recording secretary, and corresponding secretary.

Section 2. Officers shall be nominated by a nominating committee at least one month before the annual membership meeting. The nominations, with the consent of the nominees, shall be posted in the library at least two weeks prior to the annual meeting. Additional nominations may be made from the floor with the consent of the nominee.

Section 3. Officers shall be elected by a majority vote of those present at the annual meeting for the term of one year, but not more than two successive terms.

Section 4. Any vacancy occurring among the elected officers shall be filled by the vote of the members of the executive committee. Such officers shall serve for the unexpired term of his or her predecessor.

ARTICLE V. DUTIES OF OFFICERS

Section 1. President: To preside over and conduct meetings and to appoint the chairpersons of all committees and be an ex officio member thereof, except the nominating committee.

Section 2. Vice president: To perform the duties of the president in the absence of the president.

Section 3. Treasurer: To keep and maintain the financial records of the organization.

Section 4. Recording secretary: To take minutes of all meetings.

Section 5. Corresponding secretary: To keep a list of the membership, together with their addresses; to notify members of the time and place of meetings; and to conduct the correspondence of the organization.

ARTICLE VI. EXECUTIVE COMMITTEE

Section 1. The executive committee shall consist of the officers of the organization. The librarian and the chairperson of the Library's Board of Trustees shall serve as ex officio members of the executive committee.

Section 2. The executive committee shall have the authority to act on all matters on behalf of the Board of Directors between meetings of the Board.

ARTICLE VII. BOARD OF DIRECTORS

Section 1. The Board of Directors shall consist of the executive committee and the chairpersons of all committees.

Section 2. The president shall have the authority to call meetings of the Board.

Section 3. Any two members of the executive committee may request the President to call a meeting of the Board.

Section 4. The nominating committee shall consist of three members, appointed by the President: a new chairperson, the previous year's chairperson and one member from either the general membership or the Board of Directors.

Section 5. A majority of the Board of Directors shall constitute a quorum.

ARTICLE VIII. MEETINGS

Section 1. An annual meeting shall be held on a date in the month of June to be determined by the Board, at which time election of officers will take place. Notice of the time and place of the annual meeting shall be posted in the library and published in the local papers at least two weeks prior to the date of the meeting.

Section 2. Any ten members may petition the President to call an additional general meeting of the membership.

ARTICLE IX. DUES

Section 1. Dues shall be payable annually and shall become due on the day of the annual membership meeting. There shall be three classes of dues:
1. Individual—$5.00
2. Family—$10.00
3. Life Member—$50.00

Section 2. Failure to pay dues for two successive years shall constitute withdrawal of membership.

ARTICLE X. AMENDMENTS

Section 1. Amendments to these bylaws may be made at any meeting of the general membership by a two-thirds vote of those present. Notice that bylaw changes are to be voted on shall be posted in the Library and published in the local newspapers.

ARTICLE XI. FUNDS

Section 1. Fund-raising activities shall be determined by the Board of Directors and shall be subject to the approval of the Board of Trustees of the Hillsdale Library.

Section 2. Expenditures of monies shall be determined by the Board of Directors and, with the exception of administrative expenses, shall be subject to the approval of the Board of Trustees of the Hillsdale Library.

ARTICLE XII. PARLIAMENTARY PROCEDURE

Section 1. *Robert's Rules of Order* revised, when not in conflict with these bylaws, shall govern the proceedings of this organization.

Amended June 1996

FRIENDS—BYLAWS
THE FRIENDS OF THE UWM GOLDA MEIR LIBRARY

ARTICLE I: NAME

The organization shall be called: The Friends of the UWM Golda Meir Library, hereafter called "Friends."

ARTICLE II: PURPOSE

The purpose of the Friends shall be to maintain an association of persons interested in strengthening the University Library, enhancing its collections, and promoting its usefulness.

ARTICLE III: MEMBERSHIP

Section 1. All UWM students, faculty members, staff, and alumni; members of the Milwaukee community; and organizations are welcome as members of the Friends upon payment of annual membership dues.

Section 2. The classification of memberships is:

(1) Regular

(2) Contributing

(3) Sponsor

(4) Patron

(5) Corporate Benefactor

(6) Life Member (available to individuals only)

The Board of Directors of the Friends may recommend to the membership special recognition for contributions to the Friends or to the Library, including honorary life membership.

Section 3. Voting at regular and special meetings shall be by individuals present, or, in the case of votes by mail, of all eligible members. In the case of family memberships, two members of such families shall be eligible to vote. In the matter of Business/Corporate memberships, each organization shall be entitled to one vote cast by an authorized representative.

ARTICLE IV: FINANCE

Section 1. Dues are payable on or before July 1 of each year. The membership year is from July 1 to June 30. Dues for each of the various classes of membership shall be proposed by the Friends Board of Directors and ratified by the membership.

Section 2. Deposits and disbursements:

A. All dues and funds shall be made payable to the UWM Foundation—Friends of the UWM Library.

B. Contributions are tax-deductible to the extent allowed by law.

C. Expenditures must be approved by the Friends Board of Directors, and requests to the UWM Foundation to issue a check on behalf of the Friends shall be signed by two officers, one of whom is either President or Treasurer of the Friends.

D. Reports of receipts and expenditures from Friends' funds shall be given by the Treasurer at each regular business meeting. Such reports, however, shall be not less than quarterly; if regular business meetings do not occur within the allotted time, such reports shall be delivered by mail.

ARTICLE V: BOARD OF DIRECTORS

Section 1. The executive authority of the Friends shall be vested in a Board of Directors, the responsibilities and duties of whom shall include, but not be limited to: (1) raising funds by any means not expressly forbidden by these bylaws or by any law or statute; (2) allocating and expending such funds in furtherance of the purposes of the Friends; (3) recommending a schedule of dues and establishing benefits of each of the various classes of members; and (4) planning events and meetings of the membership.

Section 2. The Board of Directors shall consist of the four (4) officers of the Friends (see Article VI); the Past President; sixteen (16) Directors at large elected by the membership; two (2) Directors appointed by the UWM Alumni Association; one (1) Director appointed by the UWM Foundation; and two (2) ex officio, nonvoting members as follows: the Director of the UWM Library and the Chair of the University Library Committee.

Section 3. All Directors shall serve until the expiration of their terms except in cases of incapacity, resignation, or removal from office. An affirmative vote of two-thirds of all current members of the Board (excluding ex officio members) shall be required to remove a Director from office. The President shall, with the concurrence of the Executive Committee, have the authority to appoint a person to fill any vacancy occurring on the Board; the appointed Director shall serve until elections are held at the next scheduled annual meeting.

Section 4. The term of office for a Director at large shall be four (4) years. The terms of one-quarter of the elected Directors shall expire each year. The Past President shall serve a two-year term renewable if the current president is reelected.

Section 5. Any Director may seek reelection at the expiration of his/her first term. Directors may only serve two (2) consecutive terms, and must be off the Board for four (4) years before they may be reappointed.

Section 6. All Directors shall be elected at large by a majority of those present at the Friends Annual Meeting. The Nominating Committee shall propose a list of candidates for expiring terms and nominations shall be accepted from the membership prior to the voting.

Section 7. The President, with the concurrence of the Executive Committee, shall appoint the Chairs and members of the standing committees and the Chairs and members of any ad hoc committees as may seem appropriate. Nonmembers may not be a majority. The standing committees of the Board shall be: Communications, Development, Programs, and Nominating. The Chair of each committee will deliver a report of the committee's activities at each Annual Meeting of the Friends.

Section 8. The officers of the Board shall serve as voting members of the Executive Committee of the Board.

Section 9. All Board members, following completion of their service on the Board, shall be invited to become directors emeriti for one year following, and shall receive notification and agendas of Board meetings.

ARTICLE VI: EXECUTIVE COMMITTEE

Section 1. The executive Committee shall consist of six (6) members as follows: the four (4) officers of the Board; the Past President; and the Director of the Library, (nonvoting, ex officio).

Section 2. The duties of the Executive committee shall be to act on behalf of the Board, during the interval between board meetings, in all matters related to the operation of the Board, including, but not limited to the duties stated in Article V, Section 1, of the bylaws, except those actions requiring full Board or membership approval as specified elsewhere in the bylaws.

Section 3. Three (3) voting members of the Executive Committee shall constitute a quorum for the transaction of business at any meeting of the Committee.

ARTICLE VII: OFFICERS OF THE FRIENDS

Section 1. The officers of the Friends shall be a President, Vice President, Secretary, and Treasurer. Each officer shall serve a term of two (2) years and all officers are automatically members of the Board of Directors.

Section 2. The president shall be the chief officer of the Friends, fulfilling all of the normal duties of that office including, but not limited to, presiding at all meetings of the Board of Directors and of the membership, conducting the business of the association with the concurrence of the Board of Directors, affixing an official signature to association documents, and representing the Friends in an official capacity. At the completion of the term of office, the President becomes Past-President.

Section 3. The duties of the Vice president shall be to assist the President in the fulfillment of the latter's duties and to act on behalf of the president in the event of the latter's absence.

Section 4. The Secretary shall be responsible for maintaining the Friends records and the minutes of all Board and membership meetings, conducting all official correspondence, and compiling a list of eligible members for use in elections requiring a mail vote.

Section 5. The Treasurer shall be responsible for maintaining the financial records, certifying the accuracy of all requests for expenditure of funds, and preparing quarterly reports of income and expenses. The Treasurer shall deliver a complete annual report at the Annual Meeting of the Friends.

Section 6. The officers shall be elected at the Annual Meeting of the Friends by a majority of those present. The Nominating Committee of the Board shall present a list of at least one (1) nominated candidate for each office and nominations shall be accepted from the membership during the meeting. If an elected member of the Board of Directors is elected as an officer of the Friends, his/her term as a Director is declared vacated and a new Director shall be elected to fill the term.

Section 7. The terms of the officers shall be staggered, with the President and Treasurer elected in the first year, and the Vice president and Secretary elected in the following year.

Section 8. All officers shall serve until the expiration of their terms except in cases of incapacity, resignation or removal from office. An affirmative vote of two-thirds of all current members of the Board (excluding ex officio members) shall be required to remove an officer from office for cause. The Board shall have the authority to appoint a person to fill any vacancy occurring through resignation, incapacity, or removal from office on an interim basis until the next Annual meeting. If such a person, selected to act on an interim basis, is a current officer, he/she must resign that office and the Board must elect a person to fill that vacancy; if such a person is a current elected Director, he/she must take a leave of absence from the Directorship, and the Board must elect a person to fill that vacancy until the interim appointment expires.

ARTICLE VIII: MEETINGS

Section 1. Unless otherwise authorized by the Board of Directors, the annual election of Directors, biennial election of officers, and business meeting of the membership will be held in the spring of each year on a date to be determined by the Board of Directors.

Section 2. A quorum for conducting business at the Annual Meetings shall be defined as those persons present at such meetings.

Section 3. The Board of Directors shall meet at least twice each year and at other times as called by the President or by any five (5) Directors, one of whom must be an officer of the Friends, or by petition of 10% of the membership.

Section 4. All meetings shall be conducted according to Roberts Rules of Order (Revised).

ARTICLE IX: AMENDMENTS TO THESE BYLAWS

These Bylaws may be amended at the Annual Meeting of the Friends, or at a special meeting called by petition of 10% of the membership, by a two-thirds vote of those members present or by a two-thirds vote of all eligible members voting by a mail vote, provided that

notice of such proposed amendments is mailed to all members at least two weeks before said meeting or the deadline of such mail vote.
Revised May 23, 2000.

B PRE-NUPTIALS AMONG FRIENDS: SPELLING OUT WHAT THE FRIENDS GROUP WILL (AND WILL NOT) DO

Some will look at this page and say, "Wait! You already have a constitution and bylaws, why do you need this?" This is a good question and the answer is simple, even obvious. But as Samuel Johnson once said, "What is obvious is not always known, and what is known is not always present." So, here goes.

If you look back over the sample Constitution (see Appendix A), you will notice there's little in it about how the friends group continues each year. Sure, there are serving terms for those in administrative roles but nothing about longevity. Much of what is said here comes under the heading of "Preventive Medicine" or "Preventive Maintenance."

1. Offer a diversity of programming. You want programs that appeal to everyone, or nearly everyone. Any given program will not, of course, do this, so you need to have a variety of programs, appealing to every type of user. It serves as a good reminder that the friends group is really pluralism at its best, and this includes programming and outreaches for all, in the same way that your library's services seek to do the very same. You can do this by scheduling a book author one year, a fun-run the next. If you're really ambitious, do both, one in the spring and one in the fall. By doing this you make certain that each program will probably bring in new members. It also generates a publicity excitement: "What will they think of next?"

But this is not the only debilitating part of a single-minded group. Your membership is exhausted in different ways. Either they come to the event and then are ready to go on to another activity, or they do not attend and are "conditioned" to ignore the next advertisement about a friends program. Either way, you have inevitably cut off your ready-made audience. Would-be members are also conditioned into thinking that this is not for them. Before long, you find that attendance to these affairs is limited to the same three or four dozen couples every time. This will get the friends group nowhere fast, and off to the tar pits faster than the brontosaurus.

It makes eminently better sense to schedule events of wide appeal. If there are those in your membership who really do want to invite the local "poet laureate" to recite her doggerel, let them do so, but not under the aegis of the friends. In the same way that Microsoft is careful about its name, so must you be careful about what your friends group becomes associated with. It must be about programs with wide appeal, and community-wide reach. It is silly to think that *every* program will draw a large crowd. But many will if they are positioned in such a way, not as culture-lite, or as culture-dense, but as the events that speak well of your group and of your efforts.

2. Establish your program as part of all other existing programs within your larger organization. Almost without warning, groups can become so insular, or so sensitive that they want special treatment, special provisions and special allowances not made elsewhere within your organization. Perhaps this occurs after some real or perceived offense, or because a given program or event requires special allowances in order for it to be successful. *Sometimes* these can be made through the proper channels. But all too often they cannot. Feelings are hurt, resentment arises and situations become fraught with unnecessary tension. It doesn't matter who is right and who is wrong (it takes two to tango), only that this "problem" stands between the friends group and its success. Better to prevent its possibility than have to deal with it later.

3. Organize your group to buy library materials. Left to their own devices, ninety-nine out of one hundred times, the friends group will organize to buy the library books alone. This is especially the case if the friends group is organizing around an academic library. On the surface this seems like a great idea. Generally speaking, librarians of *any* stripe are so happy to have any kind of interest that the temptation to allow for exclusive purchase of one type of library material is allowed. The librarian may be thinking, "I'll deal with that later." It is almost irresistible, because many new friends groups organize around this common theme anyway. I can tell you only what twenty years of experience has taught me: resist the temptation.

Surely this must sound like looking a gift-horse in the mouth, but if you are an effective friends coordinator, you must look at all your patrons, not just one segment of them. In cases where one group focuses on purchasing books alone, you need to establish yet another group to tackle these broader needs, or leave them unmet. It is far better to establish the group as a fund-raising arm of the library, not the only fund-raising *finger* of your library.

Your library offers *services*, plural, not a service. A librarian asked to offer only one service would rightly howl at the suggestion (not to mention bristle). No more then should you allow your friends group to buy only a single material. It is unlikely they will be able to buy all you need. If they can, what then? Will they disband? It is better to have a clear understanding from the beginning.

4. Establish the Director (or Dean) as the de facto head in addition to the Friends Coordinator. Some groups will constitute themselves, set a charter and then bring you their group ready-made. Again, at first blush this seems like the best of all possible worlds. Think again.

While it may begin that way, shortly after its constitution, members will be in your office making various demands, or presenting you with sundry needs. Since this is going to happen *regardless* of how it is organized, it is better to be the *de facto* head, so you can have some say-so in what programs are put on, and when. If you fail to do this, you will forever be playing catch-up with the group. I know of one group that set itself up, planned a program, invited the speaker, and sent out invitations. It occurred when the director could not attend, during a week when many other events conflicted, and at a price that most, including library staff, could not afford.

Such are just the beginning of your problems when the director of the library is not the head of the group. Because such groups often promise to buy only books picked by its members, there is the additional logistical time involved hunting for just the right title, and so on. In other words, you are left with the headaches common to such groups, without any control. In addition to these matters, there are the less obvious ones about pressing, but nonbook-related needs unfulfilled. Forced to find funds for other needs, *someone* on staff will have to run a parallel "friends" group to handle the needs that the existing one will not. Invariably, one day the two groups will collide with each other. While the collision may not be anything other that happenstance, it will not be an affable head-on.

5. Seek Friends, not Membership Rolls. Friends groups with longevity of more than a few years make it a habit to increase the number of *friends* on their rolls, not the number of members. Groups that want to add names simply to be adding numbers will not survive past the first year or two, because those coming on board will not feel welcome. Like membership in a church, they will feel as if they have become merely a number that gets called when the budget comes due. You build donors *only* through relationships.

Of course no friends group can make *every* member feel like a true friend. But recall from the first chapter that fund-raising is as much about friends-raising as it is anything else. You can always do small things to accentuate how your members will feel about you. With your leadership, you should always be in touch every month, if not every other week. Take them to lunch, invite them to the library for coffee, or host an afternoon tea "with the library director." It need not be elaborate so much as it needs to be done. With the larger membership, try to make sure that they are on as many mailing lists about your activities as can be reasonably maintained.

Last year, for example, the library where I work and the College of Business Administration cohosted a traveling exhibit about poverty in our state. The exhibit was free, followed by a free lecture. The library provided exhibit space and had a library staff member with exhibit experience be the liaison for making sure the exhibit was up and ready on the big night. We also cohosted the reception. Library advisory board members were sent special invitations, while other friends members were notified about the event. The library stood to gain no fundraising from this event at all, nor did we want to. But we did want our members to know they were welcome and about two-thirds of them showed up. It cost us very little, both in dollars and time. Yet, the return as measured by friendship building was enormous. Events like this will go a long way in helping your group survive.

Further, if you build only a roll, you essentially build only one-time givers, *if you build even that much*. More often you will get a few curiosity seekers who will soon fall away. Word will soon circulate through the community that yours is a "numbers game," and many would-be friends will look elsewhere to spend their largess.

6. Diversify your fund-raising. Everyone invested in the stock market even on a small scale, or only through a 401(k) plan, has heard the mantra, "Diversify." Putting all your retirement eggs in one basket is one of the quickest ways to disaster when the basket tips over, as it inevitably will. This is also true about friends groups.

Friends groups generally thrive when they are not the only, or even the most important, fund-raising venture in the library. The reason this is important has to do with the cyclical nature of these groups, and that cyclical nature is not unlike the cyclical nature of the stock market. You will doubtless have some very full harvests with your friends group. Fortunately, some years you will hit upon the right theme, the right programming, or the right leadership that sends your group skyrocketing to record levels of support. Then, there are those other years.

For example, as I write these words, the stock market has been through about six months of up and down, roller coaster rising and falling prices. Because this is the case in nearly every stock market year, available funds for benevolent projects rise and fall with it. If your friends group is the only source of additional funds, you'll suffer the worst these times can give you. For us, this particular downturn has been followed by the second—some say the first—worst state funding appropriations in our state's history. It is also the same in forty-seven other states, as well. As mentioned earlier, funding for our university will have dropped twenty-seven percent by fall, 2003. So, how is it possible that we just completed a $27,000 unbudgeted project?

Mainly because we have been taking on other projects, and seeking other avenues of fund-raising, both through our friends group, through grant proposals, and through yet another group unrelated to our friends. Our success is very limited compared to what others are doing. But we simply could not be doing any of this without having made plans years ago to begin the process of diversifying our outreach.

Another reason is quite pragmatic. If all your funds come only from the friends group, and that sources dries up or is severely constricted, how do you plan programs, cover mailings and anything else you might want to do? The answer is, you cannot. Once you have cut off communication, you've just about spelled the end of your group, too. No one "best way" exists either, because all libraries are different. While we may have found success one way, another library will find success in a way in which we have failed. The trick is to try them all, or as many as you can think of, until you find the right formula.

INDEX

ACRL. *See* Association of College and Research Libraries
Adobe GoLive CS, 53
"Adventures in Wonderland," 106
advocacy groups—care, 92-93
advocacy groups—kinds, 94-95
Association of College and Research Libraries (ACRL), 10, 67
Balthaser: FX, 53
Barton College, 6
"Bittersweet Book Sale," 6
Bowling Green State University, 46, 47
Brown University, 46, 47
Bryn Mawr College Library, 46, 47
Bryn Mawr Friends of the Library, 7
Buckley, William F. Jr., 7
Cleveland Heights—University Heights Public Library, 46, 47
Cogley, Felicia, 139-140
Colorado Library of Marketing Council (CLMC), 62-63
Davidson College, 4
Dreamweaver 4.0, 53
Dreamweaver MX 2004, 53
Emmanuel School of Religion, 3
Erlichman, John, 6
"Evening with Kentucky Authors," 10
Excellence in Academic Library Awards, 10
eZediaMX 3.0, 53
Fireworks MX2004, 53
FOLUSA, viii, 9, 13, 67, 78, 101
friends bylaws, 147-150
friends groups:
  alternative resources, 30
  blogs, 81
  branding, 63-64
  communication, 41-42, 75-78
  e-mail, 79
  e-zines, 81-82
  feasibility studies, 120-124
  getting started, 17
  grants and foundations, 36-37

friends groups (*continued*)
  listserv, 79-81
  longevity, 138-141
  marketing, 62-72
  newsletters, 82-85
  strategic resources, 29-30
Friends of the Brooklyn College Library, 7
Friends of the Courtright Memorial Library—Otterbien College, 9
Friends of the E.W. King Library, 6
Friends of the Hastings, Nebraska Public Library, 139-140
Friends of the Hillsdale Library—bylaws, 150-153
Friends of the Library, North Carolina State University, 3
Friends of the Library of Collier County, 106
Friends of the Library, Ponte Vedra Beach, 106
Friends of the Library USA. *See* FOLUSA
Friends of the Library of Wellesley College, 10
Friends of the Los Angeles Public Library, 9
Friends of the Medford Public Library, 7
Friends of the Milwaukee Public Library, 10
Friends of the Mishawaka-Penn-Harris Public Library, 6
Friends of the Neill Public Library, 106
Friends of the Pickering, Ohio Public Library, 140-141
Friends of the Princeton University Library, 48-49
Friends of the Redwood Libraries, 66-67
Friends of the Robert Manning Strozier Library, Florida State University, 10

Friends of the San Jose Public Library, 7
Friends of the Santa Cruz Public Library, 3
Friends of the Simsbury Public Library, Connecticut, 3
Friends of the Sterling C. Evans Public Library, Texas A & M University, 5
Friends of the Tompkins Public Library, 5
Friends of the University of Milwaukee, Wisconsin Golda Meir Library—bylaws, 153-158
Friends of the Welles-Turner Library, 138-139
Friends of the Westport Public Library, 7
Friends of the Whitman County Library, 106
friends programs:
   budgeting, 116-117
   deciding on the event, 107-109
   locale, 110-111
   press connections, 113-115
   publicity, 112-113
   researching the event, 115-116
   theme of, 111
   time of the event, 109-110
FrontPage 2003, 53
fundraising *do's*, 25
G. Eric Jones Friends of the Library, 8
Geisel Library, 49
goal-driven advocacy groups, 94-95
Haley, Alex, 6
Kimerer, Karla, 18
King College, 6
Koob, Katherine, 6
legislative advocacy groups, 95-97
L'Engle, Madeline, 7
Lentil Festival, 106
Levin, Lillian, 138-139
Lexington Public Friends of the Library, 10
Library Advocacy NOW!, 101
library budgets, 1, 2
Library Associates, 129
library head and friends groups, 18-20
Libraries for the Future, 101
Mabee Learning Center, 11

Medford Public Library Friends, 106
"Midnight at the Millennium," 9
Mitlin, Larry, 46
Mott, Bill, 129
needs-based advocacy groups, 97
Norfolk Public Library, 46, 48
North Carolina State University, 46, 48
Novak, Michael, 6
Ohio Wesleyan University, 6
Oklahoma Baptist University, 11
one-screen rule, 45
Origen, 18
Otterbein College, 46, 48
Parks, Leland, 4
Photovista Reality Studio, 53
Princeton University, 46, 48-49
The Princeton University Library Chronicle, 49
Public Library of Des Moines Foundation, 18
Public Library of Palo Alto, 46, 49
"Raise a Mile of Pennies," 9
Ransen Gliftic, Version 3, 53
Reade, Lisa, 140-141
Reference service, 24/7, 59, 70
Robert's Rules of Order, 149
Schlesinger, Arthur Jr., 7
Schuman, Patricia, 101
seven simple *don'ts* of friends groups, 22-25
Short, Jack, 17-18
Spring Hill College Library 46, 49
Saint Anseln College, 46, 49
Sunburst Web Workshop 2.0, 53
SWISH 2.0, 53
SWOT Analysis, 67-71
ULead MySite 2.0, 53
unconventional fundraising approaches, 3, 4, 11
University of Minnesota Libraries, 46, 50
University of Pennsylvania, 46, 50
variety of friends groups, 12
web creation software, 53
web page content—rules, 43-46
Web Workshop Pro, 53
Willis N. Hackney Library, 6

ABOUT THE AUTHOR

Mark Y. Herring is Dean of Library Services at Winthrop University in Rock Hill, South Carolina. He is the author of numerous articles in nationally-known library and non-library journals and magazines, book chapters, and six books, including *Organizing Friends Groups* (Neal-Schuman), and *The Pro-Life/Choice Debate* (Greenwood Press). His "10 Reasons Why the Internet is No Substitute for a Library" has been translated into half dozen languages and reprinted in 14 states, Canada, England, France, Germany, Egypt, China, and Australia. It is also available as a 24" x 36" poster. Herring was interviewed about the article on BBC World Radio.

Herring began working in libraries during his freshman year in college. He has worked as dean or director of libraries in Tennessee, Oklahoma and South Carolina since 1979. An avid supporter of friends groups, Herring has worked with them throughout his career, beginning one in Tennessee that brought internationally-known writers to a small, largely rural community. Herring has his Master's from the Peabody Library School of Vanderbilt University and his doctorate from East Tennessee State University.

Herring is married to the former Carol Lane, a high school English teacher, and has two grown daughters, Adriel and Areli. Areli plans on entering a library program within the year.

Herring lives in Rock Hill with his wife and four cats.